Evaluating Words Ending with 'Y'

Mastering 'Real' Everyday English

Dr Sook Hee Lee

(MEd in Educational Psychology; MEd in TESOL; PhD in TESOL)

A catalogue record for this book is available from the British Library

ISBN: 978-1-907962-95-0

Published by Cranmore Publications

www.cranmorepublications.co.uk

Praise for *Evaluating Words Ending with 'Y'*

This is a quirky, interesting, playful book that provides a very **interesting and distinctive** approach to understanding how the English language can be used to evaluate our experiences, the people we meet and the things and phenomena we encounter. It expresses the **exceptional talent that Dr Susan Lee has** for introducing **her passion for systemic functional linguistics** into very **practical, very amusing** language learning activities for those learning English as a second or foreign language – and also for speakers of English learning more about how we evaluate based on our feelings, our judgements of truthfulness and morality and our appreciation of events, performances, creations and natural phenomena. *Evaluating Words Ending with 'Y'* shows how a powerful linguistic theory can be used to produce **effective and enjoyable** language learning experiences. This is an important book by a truly scholarly teacher who has drawn on her own experience as an English language learner to empower all who read this work.

Dr Len Unsworth

Professor in English and Literacies Education
Australian Catholic University, Sydney

This book embodies a **unique** approach to describing aspects of the English language which learners often do not get taught but which are essential to function effectively in an English-speaking environment. The application of the appraisal model of evaluative language in resources for language learners **is novel**, and the focus on words ending in –y allows **a surprisingly wide range of commonly-used evaluative** terms to be introduced and exemplified.

Professor Geoff Thompson

Honorary Senior Fellow, School of English, University of Liverpool, UK

Visiting Professor, Sun Yat-sen University, Guangzhou

Guest Professor, University of Science and Technology, Beijing

This book will be **very useful for teachers and learners alike**. The author has identified a very interesting area of language that will make users sound more natural and takes their vocabulary to places most **coursebooks have previously ignored**.

Richard Pincus

Head of teaching at the Embassy Language Centre, Sydney, Australia

This book is well written and fun to read. I strongly recommend it to those who want to develop a **critical ability** in English speaking and writing.

Dr Xinghua Liu

PhD (Reading, UK)

Lecturer of Applied Linguistics, Shanghai Jiao Tong University, China

Evaluating Words Ending with 'Y' is **really interesting** and provides **essential and crucial** knowledge for those who are studying English.

Haneul Lee

An international university student from South Korea

TABLE OF CONTENTS

Acknowledgements

With the deepest gratitude firstly I wish to thank God for guiding me through constant inspiration and personal revelation. I also deeply express my gratitude to the following people for their magnificent support and contribution to the production of this book.

Gratitude goes to the Embassy teachers, including the Director Carolyn Matthews who generously allowed me to conduct a survey with willing cooperation. In particular, special thanks should be given to the Embassy teachers Richard Pincus, Antoine Burke, Dominic Chellet, Angelika Maag and Jenny Barreiros for sharing their ideas and for reading through the draft and providing valuable feedback.

I would like to thank my PhD supervisor Professor Len Unsworth for providing a terrific book review despite his extremely busy schedule. I am most grateful to Professor Geoff Thompson for providing insightful comments and a wonderful book review. Thanks to the following SFL scholars for their encouragement and support on my scholarly journey: Professor Jim Martin, Dr Peter White, Dr Sally Humphrey, Dr Susan Hood, Dr David Rose and Helen Drury.

I acknowledge my lovely students and friendly colleagues at Charles Sturt University Sydney, and also my supervisor Dr Jeff Gosper and Director Sue Bakir for their support and for allowing me to use all the resources that were required for getting this book to the publication stage.

I appreciate the magnificent people who always generously proofread for me: John Magin, who is a teacher at Lloyd College, and Tiger Wise, an editor as well as In Wha Kim, who helped to design the cover.

I am also grateful to my PhD friend Dr Xinghua Liu who introduced me to my publisher and also to the team at Cranmore Publications who were interested in and dedicated to publishing my book.

And finally to my daughters, Mee-Jin Lee, Mee-Eun Lee and son Jong-do Lee, who illuminate every breath I take through their very existence, and to my husband Dr Il Kyu Lee for his support and trust in me.

✎ Test yourself!
Commonly used words that end in 'Y'

Please read through the following expressions containing commonly used words that end in 'Y' to see how many you know and use in everyday conversation. Simply tick the relevant column. If you tick less than 10 boxes in Column 1 then you need to consider buying this book.

	Column 1	Column 2	Column 3
	I know and use it in everyday conversation	I understand but I never use it	I don't know the expression
She is a very **bossy** woman.			
My neighbour tends to be **snobby.** They do not like to mix with people from other backgrounds.			
My 5-year-old boy is very **fussy.** He does not eat any vegetables.			
My husband is a very **finicky** person, while I am quite **laidback.**			
He's got a **quirky** sense of humour. Not everyone finds his jokes funny.			
Children usually get very **cranky** when they are not fed.			
He is very **grumpy** today for some reason.			
She is very **stingy.** She only gave me a card for my birthday.			
He is such a **jolly** guy.			
That mechanic is pretty **dodgy.**			
She is very **nasty.** So everyone hates her.			
He looks so **geeky** with those thick glasses he wears.			
There are all these **brainy** people at university.			
She usually wears **tacky** clothes.			
When the alarm bell rings, don't get all **panicky.**			
There are some pretty **freaky** people on Oxford Street on a Saturday night.			
It is very **fiddly** to make this kind of jewellery. You need very steady hands.			
Total			

How many boxes did you tick in Column 1?

1-5 (   )   6-10 (   )   11-15 (   )   More than 15 (   )

I. Introduction: My secret to understanding and speaking like a native

Have you ever listened to an English conversation, and a pounding storm of unfamiliar words have swirled around your head and left you with a big headache and an even bigger question: 'Will I ever understand and speak English like a native???'

As a Korean migrant to Australia at the age of 35, I regularly experienced this headache; at times it turned to heartbreak. I asked myself this question many, many times. Shortly after arriving in Australia, I contracted Lymphoid Tuberculosis largely due to the stress I experienced from the financial challenges of migrant life and my inability to express myself. I subsequently underwent two major operations and after almost two years, I finally recovered from the illness. When I had this disease, I felt like my life was over. Many years later, I completed a Master's course in TESOL (Teachers of English to Speakers of Other Languages) at the University of Wollongong, then a PhD in TESOL at the University of Sydney. I now tutor students from 60 nationalities both at undergraduate and postgraduate level at Charles Sturt University in Sydney, and have taught numerous EAP (English for Academic Purposes) as well as IELTS (International English Language Testing System) courses in colleges in Sydney over the past 7 years. I have become a well-known scholar in my field of academic writing, publishing numerous papers in prestigious journals and books worldwide (see the references at the back of the book). I am a reviewer of the Journal of US-China Foreign Language and Sino-US English Teaching and am on the Editorial Board of the TESOL Journal, a sister journal to the Asian EFL Journal. I am also a member of the Association for Academic Language and Learning (AALL) and the Australian Systemic Functional Linguistics Association (ASFLA). I am a regular columnist in the Korean Top Weekly Newspaper, which has been published in Sydney since 2008.

My three children, who have all grown up in Australia from a young age and speak like natives, affectionately tease me at times about being an English teacher since, for the most part of their lives, they have known me as a stumbling English learner. When I arrived in

Australia in 1991, I could barely speak a word of English. Now, that big question, once filled with doubt and fear, has been answered: YES! I CAN understand and speak English like a native! And if I can, you can too!

Here is my secret: Whether it is professional or casual conversation, native English speakers love abbreviating long expressions into short phrases by placing 'y' at the end. This is probably the reason why 'textbook' English will not help in understanding and using 'real' English – the words used in everyday conversation by native English speakers. An example is '**bossy**', which is used when someone's behaviour is authoritative or overbearing. It comes from the word 'boss', which is more familiar to English learners as the word used for a person with authority. Other examples, albeit from different roots, include breakfast – **brekky**, television – **telly**, football – **footy**.

My assumption about this gap between 'real' English and 'textbook' English was proven when I conducted a preliminary survey on the use of words ending in 'y'. The participants were ESL (English as Second Language) students studying English at an English Language Centre in Sydney. I used the same test that appears at the front of this book (see page 8).

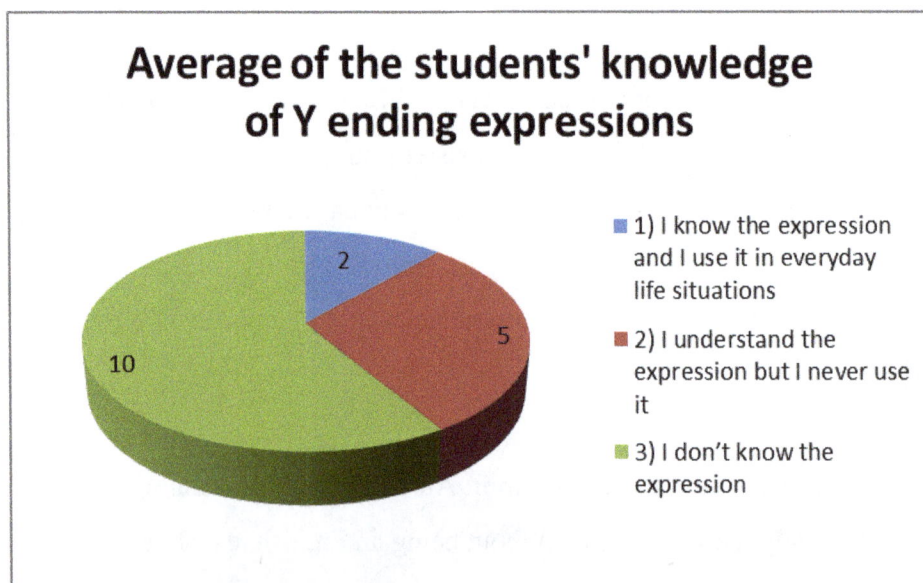

Average of the students' knowledge of Y ending expressions

- 2
- 5
- 10

1) I know the expression and I use it in everyday life situations

2) I understand the expression but I never use it

3) I don't know the expression

A total of 74 students from 6 different levels of English classes participated in the survey. The English classes were EAP 1 (8), II (9), III (11), Advanced (8), Upper Intermediate I (10) and II (11). While their length of stay in Australia varied, the average was approximately 4 months. The majority of the students were from Vietnam, South Korea, China and Colombia.

The students were required to rate 17 examples of evaluative words ending in 'Y' in accordance with three levels of its usage (see the Pie Chart above). The results of the survey revealed that **the students knew and used only 2 expressions out of 17 on average** (Category 1). Category 2 represents the gap between linguistic competence and performance. On average, the students scored 5 out of 17. When it comes to Category 3 the average student score was 10 out of 17. This means that most ESL students do not know these expressions at all. When combining categories 2 and 3 (5 + 10 = 15), we need to conclude that this book is **very useful as the students barely knew the expressions.**

There seems to be little link between the length of stay in an English-speaking country and the level of knowledge of these expressions. The results clearly demonstrate that the vast majority of ESL students are not familiar with Y ending evaluative language, irrespective of how long they have lived in an English-speaking country.

This book explains the key principles involved in oral communication and how to apply them in the casual conversation that is used in everyday life situations. The practical usage of casual conversation is confined to the evaluations that end in Y (e.g. cranky, fussy, quirky, bossy, etc), which I have documented for the past 20 years that I have lived in Australia. The principle side of the theoretical framework used in the book arises out of my PhD research which was conducted at the University of Sydney.

II. Why this book is unique

I believe that this book will be extremely useful for ESL/EFL students. This is because there are several features that distinguish this book from other casual conversation teaching materials.

✓ Firstly, in order to explain basic principles that govern oral communication, this book takes one of the models derived from the **Systemic Functional Linguistics (SFL)** approach. SFL theory was initially formulated by M.A.K. Halliday, one of the most prominent scholars in the field of linguistics. He currently holds an honorary position in the Linguistics Department at the University of Sydney. The theory is based on a socio-linguistic orientation, in contrast to Chomsky's psycho-linguistic orientation. SFL frameworks are one of the most popular pedagogies used in enhancing English literacy in Australia and England. Based on Halliday's (1994) broad notion of interpersonal resources such as speech functions, modality, and attitudinal lexis, a new theory termed **'appraisal'** has been developed by his followers such as Jim Martin, Peter White and Rick Iedema working at the University of Sydney. They were involved in the Write it Right project sponsored by the NSW Department of Education (Write it Right, 1996).

The appraisal theory is basically concerned with evaluative language. One of the main reasons we use language is to evaluate people's behavior and things as well as expressing our feelings and emotions. Taking a simple example, when we say, 'Sydney is *beautiful*', we make a positive assessment about Sydney which is a thing. When we say, 'she is so *mean*', we make a negative evaluation on the person. The theory is used as a framework for examining the use of evaluative words in casual conversation (please read details in Section 1). One of the primary tenets of the SFL approach is that context is critical when examining the use of language. In this book, the context is casual conversation in Australian English. However, I am sure that most expressions are universally used in English-speaking countries such as America, the UK, Canada and New Zealand. The focus of this book is to put the appraisal theory into practice by theorizing the casual conversation that is used in everyday life situations. As far as I know, no other book has used the theory to explain how oral communication works.

✓ Secondly, in this book I collate adjectival expressions that end in/with 'Y'. While I was living in Wollongong for 8 years, I had many opportunities to meet local Australians. During this time I was exposed to the expressions that ordinary native English speakers use in everyday life situations. I have been compiling these expressions for almost 20 years.

✓ Thirdly, what is common among the 'Y' expressions chosen here is that they are all part of the evaluative language of the **ATTITUDE** system which is part of the Appraisal theory. To put it simply, one of the main reasons why people use (the English) language is to express their subjective opinions and views about things and people. This involves **evaluating things** positively or negatively (e.g. The movie is fantastic, this room is messy), **evaluating people's behavior** (he is kind, she is a liar), and **expressing emotions and feelings** (I feel happy, I feel tired). This expression is called **ATTITUDE**. After I complete my PhD, I realised that the Y ending evaluations can fit neatly into the **ATTITUDE** system. This book focuses on the **ATTITUDE** system.

There are two main reasons why it is very important to compile a list of evaluative language ending in Y using the **ATTITUDE** system. Firstly, the expressions sound simple and easy in English but when they are translated into the students' native languages, these expressions become lengthy and complicated. Secondly, as my PhD results reveal and teachers of English acknowledge, learners find it difficult to develop their critical stance in relation to others. This is because ESL/EFL learners, in particular from Asian backgrounds, are from so called 'Communication Reticent Cultures' where expressing their opinions or views is suppressed to some degree. The Y expressions will enable them to articulate their attitude succinctly and confidently in an appropriate context.

This collection of evaluative language will also help students to keep abreast of the recent emphasis on the importance of having 'emotional intelligence' and "I feel statements" (Burns, 2008, p.134) which are thought to be necessary for successful communication in any relationship. This book has focused on teasing out the nature of communication from a linguistic perspective.

✓ Fourthly, this book also covers many other similar collocations of Y endings that can be usefully employed in slightly different contexts. This means that students will be able to learn additional synonyms that are used by native English speakers for effective communication. The examples of Y ending expressions and other relevant expressions provided here have been gathered from various sources to reflect both current and historical usage. I have included as many authentic or relevant uses of the language as possible.

✓ Finally, the book also includes grammar exercises in areas where, based on my teaching experience, many ESL/EFL learners are most prone to making errors. Learning '**speech grammar**' is important, as it is an effective approach for general language proficiency (Donaldson, 2011). The speech grammar, of course, can be transferable to the grammar required in writing. Learners will find it much easier to communicate with native English speakers once they have mastered the expressions ending with 'Y', together with other expressions and grammar pertaining to the 'Y' evaluative language. While this book deals with a survival level of spoken English, learners will notice that their writing skills will also have improved significantly.

III. Why I devoted myself to writing this book

There are three main factors that have motivated me to write this book.

- ✓ Firstly, I wanted to introduce a theory that can fit in the Y ending expressions and demonstrate how it applies to oral communication in a casual conversation context.

- ✓ Secondly, I wanted to introduce the appraisal theory and demonstrate how it can be used to address the issue of effective communication. Within SFL, this book uses the appraisal theory as a framework to teach the English language. There are some textbooks currently on the market that cover evaluative language. Therefore, this book is not something new with regards to this. However, unlike the existing conversation books published so far, all these evaluative expressions are organized based on the rigorous framework of the 'Appraisal system' formulated within Systemic Functional Linguistics (SFL) theory. The appraisal system has come to be highly regarded in Australia and England. Some American scholars have also begun to show interest in the theory.

The pedagogical approach used here is **newly developed and yet it is very simple, pragmatic, and comprehensive. This means that students can easily understand it without any prior knowledge of language learning if they are willing to take some time digesting it**. My humble wish is that at the end of the day, this book will help to motivate students to learn English in an enjoyable way, while also providing knowledge of underlying theory.

- ✓ Thirdly, I feel that I have a compelling message to convey through this book and that my unique background enables me to be a 'gap filler'. As I said earlier, I have been an English learner for 20 years and a teacher for 7 years. I learned English throughout my 10 years schooling in South Korea, but I did not learn spoken English. After arriving in Australia, I spent another 10 years leaning to speak English. Since then I have been teaching English for 7 years. This unique background allowed me to notice a gap between the original culture and the target culture that has impacted on the ways of communication; there are big gaps between learners' existing knowledge and the new requirements. That is, there is a gap between Western audience expectations and students' real abilities to cope with communication when students make transitions. Despite my deep knowledge of English vocabulary, I did not know real colloquial English such as the expressions ending in Y. Most students wish to learn English quickly and efficiently, given time and financial constraints. The importance of effective oral communication skills is equally important for university students because it greatly enhances their employability (Jones & Polly, 2013). This book is designed to bridge the gap.

While this book cannot be a panacea for mastering English, it will certainly provide a missing link between ESL/EFL learners' oral proficiency and the real English that is required to survive in English-speaking countries. Now ESL/EFL learners will be motivated to learn English not just in a rote-learning manner. English conversation skills can thus be acquired in an effective and enjoyable way.

IV. Target audience

This book targets a number of audiences.

- ✓ Adult EFL students: This book will be useful for EFL (English as a Foreign Language) students because it provides exposure to real casual expressions by offering a short-cut, enabling them to readily understand and communicate with native English speakers.

- ✓ International/ESL students/Working holiday students: It will also help ESL (English as a Second Language) students coming to English-speaking countries for work or study purposes. These students need to integrate into society within a short period of time by obtaining native like fluency in conversation. For instance, many ESL students arrive in English-speaking countries such as Australia, America, Canada and England under working holiday visas. I hope that this book will help facilitate the assimilation of those new arrivals into society as effectively as possible.

- ✓ Migrants living in English-speaking countries: The audience for this book includes anyone who wants to improve their English-speaking skills, and this includes migrants already living in English-speaking countries.

- ✓ Any person who is interested in learning English: Anyone who would like to improve their English-speaking skills will also benefit from this book.

V. Section overview

This book consists of four sections:

- ✓ *Section 1* briefly explains the nature of communication based on SFL's interpersonal function. This is followed by an introduction to the Appraisal theory.

- ✓ *Section 2* explains the 'ATTITUDE' system in detail by using examples, as it is a core and focal framework of the appraisal theory that underpins the book. I have tried my best to use plain English to explain the theories. However, if you are not interested in understanding theoretical frameworks, you can skip Sections 1 and 2. I hope readers do not feel intimidated by the theories.

- ✓ *Section 3* demonstrates the application of the ATTITUDE system to casual conversation on the basis of these frameworks. The section also contains grammar exercises and other similar expressions to the Y evaluations.

- ✓ *Section 4* compiles other types of collocations and abbreviations pertaining to the group of expressions ending in Y.

Section 1: Theory of Communication from SFL

1.1. Two main reasons why we use English

According to a Systemic Functional Linguistics (SFL) approach to language, language is used for communicating with each other from an interpersonal perspective (Halliday, 1994; Eggins, 2000; Halliday & Matthiessen, 2004; Thompson 2013). This means that the most important reason why learners are keen to learn English is to have successful communication with others. Communication can take place for the purpose of achieving two main goals (see Figure 1). One goal is to 'interact' with people when exchanging information and goods & services (**Interaction**).

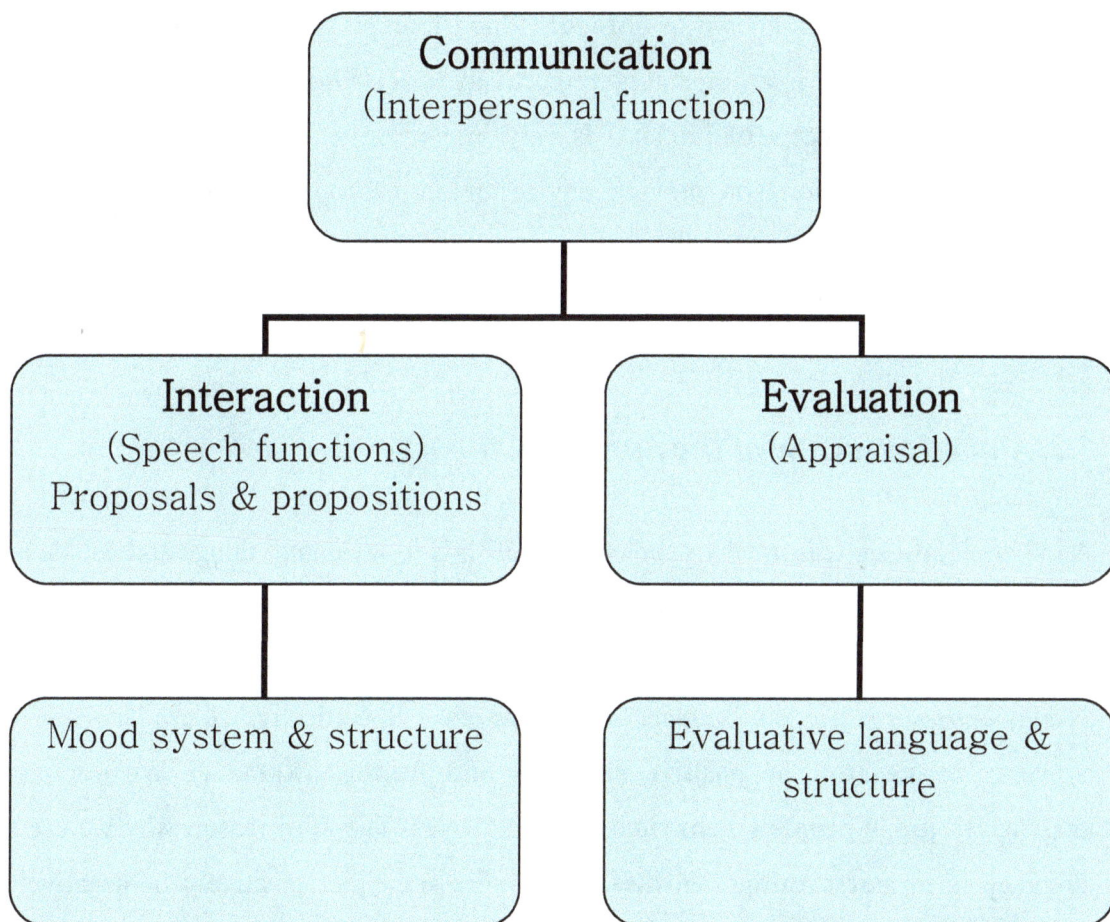

Figure 1: Two main reasons for communication

When speakers would like to **exchange information,** they mostly use questions that contain six prompts of WH questions: what, when, why, how, where, and who (e.g. where are you from?) and then listeners respond to the speakers by using statements (e.g. I come from China). When speakers want to **exchange goods and services,** they make a request by using questions (e.g. Can I borrow the pen? [a Good]) or commands (e.g. please send the letter to me [a Service]). That is, interaction fulfils **four speech functions or roles** of English, namely statements, questions, commands and offers. Halliday (1994) claims that when language is used to exchange information, the clause takes on the form of a **proposition, which has informational value** in the exchange. When the clause is structured to enable the exchange of goods and services, it takes the form of **a proposal, which has interactional value.** Offers and commands are thus grouped together as **proposal**, and statements and questions as **proposition** (see Figure 1). The grammar to express the functions is known as '**Mood**'. Mood is expressed in a grammar that is declarative, interrogative, or imperative respectively (see Halliday & Matthiessen, 2004; Lee, 2010a). The concept of proposal is very important in explaining how to make requests/recommendations or provide advice in an appropriate manner. From an interactional perspective, all English sentences encode either proposals (he should come) or propositions (he will come).

1.2. A brief overview of the Appraisal theory

Another significant reason why people use English is to 'evaluate' things and people as well as to express their feelings and emotions (**Evaluation**). When speakers take up such positions, they express their subjective/individual opinions or views to listeners (e.g. Sydney is *beautiful*; He is a *conman,* I am *happy,* etc.). Specifically, we use language to **express our negative or positive emotions and feelings** (AFFECT). We also use language to **judge people's behaviour** (JUDGEMENT). The third reason why we use a language is to **assess things, entities, and processes** either positively or negatively (APPRECIATION). These three functions are called ATTITUDE, because the resources reflect our attitude (see Figure 2). These three meanings of evaluations constitute the ATTITUDE system (see details, Butt et al., 2000; Martin 2000; Hood, 2006, 2010; Martin

& White, 2005/2007; Martin & Rose, 2003/2007; Lee, 2008c). People reflect their attitude when choosing positive and negative evaluative expressions. When they use the attitudinal evaluations, they demonstrate their subjective views through positive or negative affirmations. For instance, when we say, 'she is a *good* teacher' then logically, we have to justify or legitimate why we make such a judgement by using evidence (e.g. according to Jim, Jim reports that…), causes and effects (e.g. This is because…), concessions (Although she speaks slowly, she is a good teacher), etc. The main reason why we use those resources is because we consider listeners' different views or reactions. In other words, we would like to engage with listeners to persuade them. These resources are called **ENGAGEMENT.** In addition, when we make personal opinions and engage with listeners, we also scale up and down the value. For instance, 'she is an *extremely* good teacher', 'she is a *relatively* good teacher', she is a *better* teacher than others, she is *ok*, she is *so so*, etc. These resources that help to volume up and down are called **GRADUATION**. That is, appraisal consists of three sub systems termed **ATTITUDE, ENGAGEMENT** and **GRADUATION** (see Figure 2).

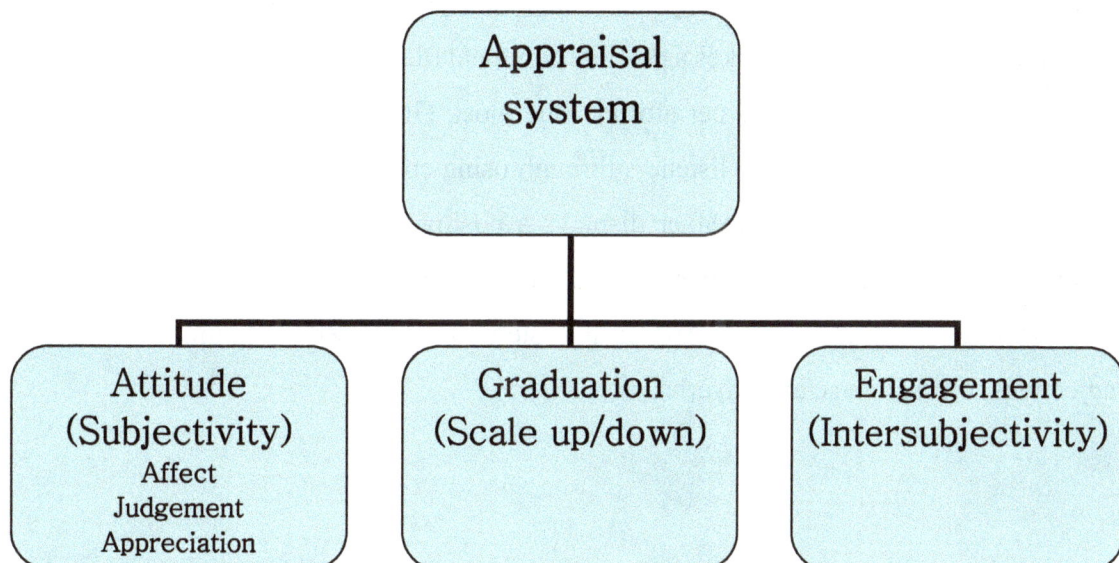

Figure 2: Three appraisal categories

In short, while we seek information and goods and services, we **simultaneously** evaluate them by expressing our attitude or taking a position. For example, the following sentence can be analysed according to the appraisal system.

Original sentence	According to a survey, Sydney is ranked as one of the most desirable cities to live in.
Appraisal analysis	*According to* a survey [Engagement; evidence], Sydney is ranked as one of *the most* [Graduation] *desirable* [Attitude: + Appreciation] cities to live in.

This analysis can be coded as follows:

ATTITUDE			ENGAGEMENT	GRADUATION
Affect	Judgement	Appreciation		
		+ desirable	According to	The most

In the sentence, the speaker not only sends the information that Sydney is a nice place to live in (Interaction) but also makes a positive comment (desirable: Attitude) about Sydney. The speaker also scales up his/her attitude (the most: Graduation) and uses an external source of statistics to convince listeners through using engagement resources (according to: Engagement). While the speaker displays a positive attitude with great conviction toward the proposition, s/he opens up negotiation simultaneously by attributing its responsibility to other sources. Appraisal systems are realised in grammar by using adjectives, verbs, nouns, and adverbs.

Section 2: An introduction to ATTITUDE and its examples

ATTITUDE is one of the three main appraisal resources and it is considered to be the most important way that speakers can convey their evaluations. Consequently, in this book, I have chosen to concentrate solely on words that help us to express our subjective attitude. However, I have restructured those expressions to adjectival words that end with 'Y'. This is because such expressions are a commonplace feature of Australian English, especially everyday spoken interaction, yet cause ESL learners considerable difficulty.

On the basis of the three types of ATTITUDE, namely Affect, Judgement and Appreciation, we use English to express our positive and negative attitude explicitly and implicitly. I will now give some examples of words/phrases that express AFFECT, JUDGEMENT and APPRECIATION (see Figure 3 below).

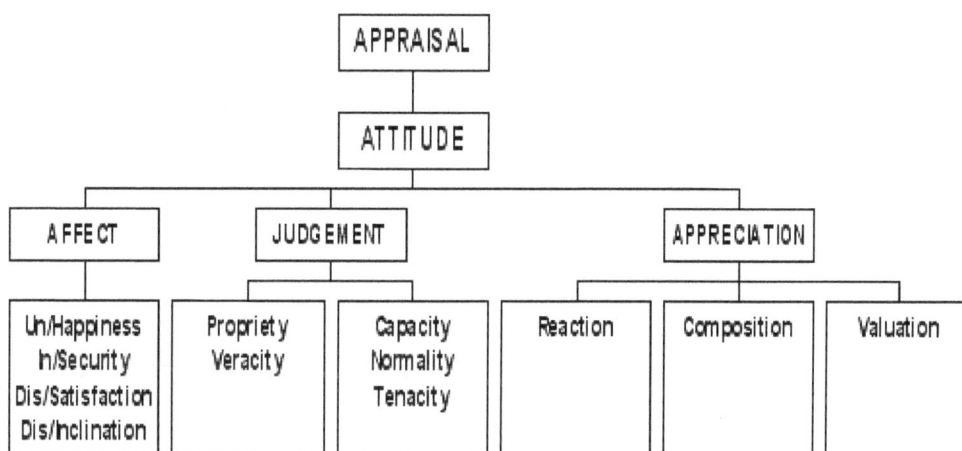

```
                    ┌───────────┐
                    │ APPRAISAL │
                    └─────┬─────┘
                    ┌─────┴─────┐
                    │ ATTITUDE  │
                    └─────┬─────┘
        ┌─────────────────┼─────────────────────┐
   ┌────┴───┐      ┌───────┴──────┐      ┌────────┴─────┐
   │ AFFECT │      │  JUDGEMENT   │      │ APPRECIATION │
   └────┬───┘      └───────┬──────┘      └────────┬─────┘
        │            ┌─────┴─────┐        ┌────────┼─────────┐
┌───────┴──────┐ ┌───┴────┐ ┌────┴────┐ ┌──┴────┐ ┌──┴───────┐ ┌┴────────┐
│ Un/Happiness │ │Propriety│ │Capacity │ │Reaction│ │Composition│ │Valuation│
│ In/Security  │ │Veracity │ │Normality│ │        │ │           │ │         │
│Dis/Satisfaction││        │ │Tenacity │ │        │ │           │ │         │
│Dis/Inclination││        │ │         │ │        │ │           │ │         │
└──────────────┘ └────────┘ └─────────┘ └────────┘ └───────────┘ └─────────┘
```

Figure 3: ATTITUDE resources within the 'Appraisal' system

Before looking at how the ATTITUDE system can be implemented in casual expressions that end in 'Y', I would like to mark them in various ways. The following table explains some symbols used in the book to indicate several ways of differentiating Y-related expressions.

Key concepts and terms	**Bold**
Key Y expressions	***Bold & Italic***
Other Y expressions	*Italic*
Word collocations of Y expressions	*Italic + Underlined*
Other related expressions, idioms and words that are useful to be learned	• Underlined with bullet points
Important speech grammar + expressions, idioms and words. These focus on the grammatical errors that ESL students make most frequently or grammars that are useful for improving conversation as well as writing The most important grammar used in Y expressions is marked with the * symbol. This indicates that it is singled out for special attention and practice in separate boxes. In these boxes the most error-prone grammar is highlighted using bold.	Underlined

Nouns that are abbreviated into a 'Y' form are listed in Section 4, and the # symbol is also used to mark these nouns in previous sections.

2.1. AFFECT

Firstly, we use English in everyday life situations to express our **emotions and feelings either negatively or positively.** This is called **AFFECT**. **AFFECT** can be sub-classified into four dimensions.

2.1.1. Un/Happiness

I felt like *jumping over the moon* when I heard the news that I got promoted.

I *feel very excited about* attending my graduation ceremony.

I am very *upset about* what has happened to me lately.

2.1.2. Dis/satisfaction

I *am full.* I cannot eat anymore.

I was *extremely tired.* I was *completely flat out.* So I *slept like a log* yesterday as soon as I went to bed.

2.1.3. In/security

I feel *at home and comfortable* living in Sydney although the city is not my home town.

I feel *terrified* at the scene of a crime/an accident.

I felt completely *freaked out* when I saw the incident.

2.1.4. Dis/inclination

This has to do with a **'potential future event'.** This is different from the three previous AFFECTs, as they involve 'reaction' to an event in **the present or past.**

I am *willing* to learn English, while he is *very reluctant* to do so.

Although the students *are eager to* engage in the activity, _____

Even though the students *are keen on* studying, _____

He *is anxious to* complete his studies as soon as possible (desire for the future-Inclination).

He is *anxious about* the exam result (reaction to the past-Affect Insecurity).

2.2. JUDGEMENT

Secondly, we use evaluative language in order to **judge people's behaviour.**
JUDGEMENT can be made on the following five aspects of human behaviour.

2.2.1. Un/ethical (Propriety)
It is related to whether a person is **ethical or unethical.**

He is a *reliable* person, because he always keeps his word.

He is a *law-abiding* person, as he always observes/follows the rules.

It is not acceptable when you *cheat* in your exam.

2.2.2. Un/truthful (Veracity)
It has to do with how the person **is truthful or honest.**

As long as she acknowledges her mistakes, she is considered to be a very *honest* person.

He is a *conman,* because_____

He is an *unscrupulous* man, because_____

My supervisor is *sneaky* and *cunning*, because_____

2.2.3. In/capable (Capacity)
We are judging how the person is **capable.**

He is very *capable of playing the piano,* because_____

He is so *dumb,* because_____

2.2.4. Ab/normal (Normality)
It *is concerned with* how **the person is usual or special.**

The girl is lovely but she is so *weird* sometimes.

Since he has an *eccentric* personality, he_____

2.2.5. Un/determined (Tenacity)
We are judging how **the person is persistent, determined or dependable.**

While he is so *determined,* he is sometimes *indecisive.*

He is *a hard worker,* but sometimes he is *not conscientious*. He is *slack.*

2.3. APPRECIATION

Thirdly, English is used to **assess or appraise things, objects, entities, products and processes,** either positively or negatively. This is called **APPRECIATION.** APPRECIATION is also divided into three aspects:

2.3.1. Un/Appealing (Reaction)

It is concerned with whether or not **the thing grabs our attention or appeals to our emotion.**

This food was so ***yummy*** that I ate it all by myself. However, I do not like eating the bread, because it tastes ***yucky***.

While the movie is *entertaining, it is a bit boring* at the beginning.

2.3.2. Un/balancing (Composition)

It <u>focuses on</u> whether or not the things or processes **have balance or not and are simple or complicated.**

Things are getting *complicated*, because_____

Students' writing is too *lengthy and messy*. So I cannot understand it.

The theory is *not systematically presented,* so it confuses me.

2.3.3. In/significant (Valuation)

It has to do with whether or not the thing **has social significance or worth**.

In order to get a job in South Korea, it is vitally *important* to <u>have a good command</u> of English.

It is crucially *essential* to speak English fluently to get a good job.

Too much use of detergent is *harmful* to the environment, because <u>it has a *detrimental* effect on waterways, plants and animals.</u>

Some key points need to be made in using ATTITUDE values. As already noted, all ATTITUDE items involve either positive or negative evaluations. It is thus very important to use evaluative language appropriately because speakers' choices make listeners react to the utterance positively or negatively too. Another key point is that it is sometimes not clear what the target of the evaluation is. It can be judging people's behavior (thus Judgement) or assessing things or processes (thus Appreciation). For instance, in the expression, "well done, good work, your work is so fabulous", here it can point to the person's ability or the work itself. There are also some overlaps among the three sub-categories of ATTITUDE. For instance, when someone is *cranky*, it can refer to the person's behavior (thus Judgement abnormality) or it can refer to the emotion (thus Affect unhappy). Another consideration is that evaluation can be explicit or implicit. For example, the sentence 'Your room is so *dirty*' is an explicit evaluation. Sometimes, evaluations can be made very subtly. Your room *is full of rubbish* (implicit or token). This means the room is not so tidy.

Most importantly, I follow the SFL approach that context is critical to conveying meaning. Consequently, the words I have chosen are words used in everyday conversation in Australia. In this context, some meaning may be surprising, but familiarity with the words will greatly advantage ESL/EFL speakers.

Summary of ATTITUDE

1. What are the three subsystems of ATTITUDE? Explain the functions of them.

2. What are the four subcategories of AFFECT? Give some positive and negative examples.

3. What are the three subcategories of JUDGEMENT? Give some positive and negative examples.

4. What are the three subcategories of APPRECIATION? Give some positive and negative examples.

Section 3: Practices of ATTITUDE in casual conversation

Unit 3.1 AFFECT
3.1.1. Un/Happiness

<u>Negative</u>

1) **Sulky**

The girl is **sulky** very often. She does not speak when she is angry at her mum.

She is in a **sulky** mood.

The dog was **sulky** because it got yelled at by his owner.

Instead she just acted like a rather **sulky** teenager, whose boyfriend had deserted her.

She looked **sulky** all morning because she was angry about <u>the way her mother told her off</u>.

- Do not take his words personally, that is <u>the way</u> he speaks to everyone.
- I was very offended by <u>the way</u> he treated me.

The girl is *sooky* and cries all the time. Leave her alone. She is *having a sook.*

2) **Cranky**

My husband is **cranky** this morning <u>for no reason</u>.

My husband has a *bad temper* and he *gets cranky* easily whenever I ask him to wash the dishes.

On my return I apologized for being so **cranky** and I guess the strain of the last couple of days was showing!

Jenn, who teaches her children at home, would become **cranky**, tired and irritable during the day.

Depending on their mood, women often tend to *feel cranky.*

- When babies need sleep, they begin to *chuck a temper tantrum.* [cf. Do not *chuck rubbish away* out of the house without considering what can be recycled].

3)   Grumpy

He is very *grumpy* today <u>for some reason</u>. He is in very *<u>low spirits</u>* today.

The guy is always *grumbling*. He needs to view things positively.

You look very *grumpy* today. What is wrong with you?

She is a bit nervous and can get a bit *grumpy* so needs to be in a home without young children or other cats.

He is a *grumpy* old man.

There are* several issues that the **grumpy** person needs to be deal with.

[Grammar 1: Relative pronouns (Embedded clauses)]

Examples:

<u>Defining</u>

There are many international students **who are** studying overseas.

There are many international students **studying** overseas.

There are many books **(that were) written** in English.

There were many books **written** in ancient Egypt.

Sample essays **(that were) written** by students are available in the library.

Sample essays **written** by students are available in the library.

<u>Non-defining</u>

Japan, which has suffered from continuous earthquakes, has been inundated with aid agencies.

Japan, suffering from continuous earthquakes, has been inundated with aid agencies.

The driver, who died instantly, was a close friend of mine.

4) Grouchy

I am sorry to be so *grouchy* today.

He has a bad temper and is very *grouchy* all the time.

Most people feel *grouchy* and uncertain about life after retirement.

Are you *grouchy* or irritable? Do you fall asleep driving? If the answer is yes, read on.

The *grouchy* teacher told the students to work from their books.

Weight loss doesn't have to be about starvation, fighting hunger pangs, resisting cravings, getting *grouchy*, lethargic, and suffering through headaches.

5) Huffy

My sister is a _control freak_. She does not take my ideas and feelings into account. If I don't do everything her way, she get very annoyed and *huffy*.

Now, don't *get huffy*. I was only _teasing._

The comedy is about a *huffy* actress who loudly protests every perceived insult, no matter how slight.

6) Whingy/whiney

My husband is always *whinging/whingy.*

He complains when I make even the smallest of mistakes.

He is always *whining.*

Stop *whinging*. [cf. There is a tendency that '*whinge*' is used in UK and Australia, '*whine*' is US].

The little puppy has been *whining* from early in the morning. He must be sick.

He is always *whingy* and blames me if things go a little wrong.

- He tends to pass the blame to me when things do not go well. He is _buck passing_.

- He _passes the buck_ when things do not turn out the way he wants.

  [cf. Buck has several meanings: a) A US, Australian or New Zealand dollar. E.g. Give me five bucks/dollars); b) I was tempted to _pass the buck_ by making someone else responsible].

He is always *whining*/complaining about the weather.

Quit *whining* and finish your dinner.

"I want to leave now," she **whined.**

The workers were **whining** that the office was too cold.

The dog was **whining** because it wanted to go out.

7)   Gloomy

You look ***gloomy/melancholy***.

You *look depressed*. Come on <u>cheer up</u>, <u>chin up</u>.

What's wrong with you? Please <u>get it off your chest</u>.

Let's <u>have a chat and talk about it</u>.

<u>Don't hold it back.</u> Don't <u>bottle it up.</u>

You need to let it out. Otherwise, you <u>get stressed</u> and it makes you become sick <u>at the</u> <u>end of the day</u>.

8)   Moody

Teenagers are famous for being ***moody***.

He is so ***moody***. He makes me *feel rather down.*

I don't like men who are ***moody***. He *suffers from depression*.

Whenever he feels depressed, he has severe <u>mood swings.</u>

Sometimes he is up and then his mood goes down abruptly.

When <u>you</u> <u>are up</u>, you are <u>in a good mood</u> and you feel excited or joyful. When you <u>are</u> <u>down</u>, you are <u>in a bad mood</u>. You head hangs low, your shoulders sag and you might feel like crying.

9)   Mushy

That was a ***mushy*** love story. The movie was so romantic that I felt sentimental.

Cook until the fruit is soft but not ***mushy***. I do not like ***mushy*** food.

The peach was overripe and ***mushy/soft***.

The bottom of the pond is all ***mushy***/*wet* and feels awful when you stand up.

Take care not to overcook them as the flesh will become ***mushy.***

Mushy stuff; no *crunchy* stuff for me.

10) Teary

I become very ***teary/tearful*** when I am watching a <u>soapie</u>#.

[cf Soapie is an abbreviation of soap operas. Australians use 'soapie' and Americans use 'soaps'/'soap'. It refers to TV dramas. Most Asians love to watch Korean soap operas (soapies)]. I love dramas/<u>soapies</u>. Korean soap operas/soapies/dramas are so fun. Once you watch them, you <u>stay glued </u>all day long. They are <u>hooked on</u> the dramas.

Kids love to watch the <u>telly</u>#/television**.** They are <u>hooked on</u> the Simpsons.

Watching the <u>telly</u> can become <u>addictive</u>.

- They <u>stay glued</u> once they begin to watch it. It <u>becomes addictive</u>.

- They <u>are addicted to</u> Korean dramas. They become Korean <u>drama addicts</u>.

- When they watch them, they cry <u>as if they are in the same situation</u> as the main characters.

11) Weepy

The teenagers got all ***weepy*** near the end of the film.

She started getting ***weepy*** when she talked about her mother.

I am ***weepy*** enough that I even cry at happy endings to movies and books.

He says he doesn't feel like going out with his friends and he is quite ***weepy*** a lot of the time.

Laura, with eyes still red and ***weepy***, said, 'It isn't mine'.

Other days, she was depressed, exhausted, ***weepy,*** aggressive, irritable, dulled.

- When I hear that his parents <u>passed away</u>, I *take pity on* him.

- I am sorry to hear that. I feel sorry for him. [cf. When he heard the bad news, he <u>passed out</u>/fainted]. <u>Commiseration</u>.

12) Sappy/soppy

They easily become ***sappy*** and cry with little reason.

I feel ***soppy/sappy***/sentimental whenever I listen to a love song.

I love to listen to ***soppy*** love songs.

Sometimes, I enjoy <u>listening</u>* to sad music. (See the box below for further grammar exercises in using an '-ing form after certain transitive verbs).

[Grammar 2: Transitive verbs that require an '-ing form]

Most transitive verbs are followed by both *-ing* form and 'to infinitive'.

Examples:

I begin to do this/ I begin doing this.

I continue to do this/ I continue doing this.

However, the following transitive verbs require only 'ing form:

We **delayed/postponed** <u>launching</u> the product because of technical problems.

I **look forward to** <u>meeting</u> you next week.

I don't **mind** <u>staying</u> late.

I really **enjoy** <u>travelling</u> abroad.

I have **finished** <u>doing</u> my assignments.

Students should **avoid** <u>plagiarizing</u> other work.

I **considered** <u>quitting</u> my job.

I will **stop** gambling.

I **quit** doing the work.

Positive

13)   Jolly

Santa Claus is a typical example of a *jolly* person.

My son is always a *jolly* guy. He looks cheerful.

He used to be a *happy* and *jolly* guy but because he is going through puberty, he is *grumpy* all the time.

Goodbye my love. I wish you had been here last night. We had an awfully *jolly* evening.

Jolly good chaps; let's go fight in the mountains of Afghanistan.

After the service, a very *jolly* ' tea ' party was held in the village hall, which was much enjoyed by all who attended.

14)   Smiley

She is always *smiley*. She always *has a smile on her face*.

Show your *smiley* face when I see you next time.

(cf. *Smileys* are also known as "emoticons". They are glyphs used to convey emotions in your writing. They are a great way to brighten up posts. 😃)

- You are bright and *chirpy* this morning [cf. The birds are chirping].

This area has been left deliberately blank for you to make notes or add other words.

Notes for Un/Happiness

3.1.2. Dis/satisfaction

Negative

15)   Weary

I become so **weary**, because he <u>keeps interrogating</u> me about the case. I *feel drained*.

She completely *wears me out*.

I need to rest my **weary** eyes.

The miners were **weary** after a long shift.

She was **weary** from years of housework.

16)   Achy

I feel all **achy.**

I have an **achy** back.

By evening I was beginning to feel restless and had really **achy** thighs so I had a bath with clary sage burning in the background.

When you catch a cold, you suffer from symptoms such as a runny nose, cough and temperature. You may feel **achy**.

I have **achy** feet by wearing shoes which are light, comfortable fitting and flexible.

17)   Stuffy

When I go into a small house, I feel very uncomfortable because the house is a **stuffy** space/place.

Open the car window. I feel sick. The car is very **stuffy.**

The swelling and fluid caused by blood and lymph vessel swelling <u>results in</u>* the symptoms of **stuffy** nose and *watery* eyes. (See the box below for further grammar exercises in cause and effect. This aspect of grammar is very important and yet students often find it difficult).

[Grammar 3: Causes and effects (ENGAGEMENT: Claim)]

- The government lowered the speed limit to 50 Km per hour. <u>As a result/as a consequence/consequently</u>, the number of traffic deaths decreased.

- The lowering of the speed limit to 50 Km per hour **resulted in** a decrease in the number of traffic deaths.

- The lowering of the speed limit to 50 Km per hour **led to** a decrease in the number of traffic deaths.

- The lowering of the speed limit to 50 Km per hour was the **cause of** the decrease in the number of traffic deaths.

- The lowering of the speed limit to 50 Km per hour was the **reason for** the decrease in the number of traffic deaths.

- The lowering of the speed limit to 50 Km per hour **had an effect on** the decrease in the number of traffic deaths.

- Recent climate change **has affected** people and nature in countless ways.

- Pollution in the air **has had a detrimental effect on** the environment.

- Recent climate change **has influenced/impacted (on)** people and nature in countless ways

- Recent climate **change has had an influence/impact on** people and nature in countless ways.

As the weather warms, spending *sunny* afternoons in a **stuffy** art museum hurts.

A **Stuffy** nose is caused by low oxygen in cells. Natural remedies are avoidance of allergies and breathing exercises.

Nasal congestion or '*stuffy* nose' occurs when nasal tissues and blood vessels become swollen with excess fluid, causing a **stuffy** feeling.

[cf. I have bought lots of stuff. I love this stuff/thing].

- You feel very frustrated when you can hardly express yourself in English (in other language 'stuffy' implies frustration).

18)   Dizzy

I have low blood pressure. That is why I get **dizzy** easily.

When you catch a cold, you get **dizzy** and get a headache.

Another major symptom is that you have a *runny* nose.

My nose is *runny*. I sneeze a lot. I am very *sneezy*.

- I need to take a sickie[#].
- How come you did not go to work today?

  I am having a sickie today. [cf. 'Sickie' is an abbreviation of 'sick leave'. Australians can be entitled to apply for a sickie once a month. Strictly speaking, the terms 'sickie' and 'sick leave' are different from each other. Sickie is used when you are not sick but pretend to be sick. Sick leave is used when you are genuinely sick. When taking sick leave, the person must bring a doctor's certificate].

- I am on study leave. I have deferred my study, because I have to go to the army. To serve at the army is obligatory, mandatory, and compulsory. Nobody can get away from it. It is unavoidable. So I put off my study for two years.
- You can't get away from doing this, you must do it.

19)   Dozy/drowsy

If you feel **drowsy** while driving from city to city, stop the car, get out and stretch your legs.

Too much alcohol can make you feel **drowsy**.

I feel very **drowsy** when I take this pill.

The boy was so *drowsy* because his mathematics class was boring.

I felt *drowsy* after my long trip to the office.

We spent a *drowsy* afternoon by the pool.

I feel very tired. I slept late yesterday. So I slept in this morning.

I feel very *sleepy* today. So I nodded off when I attended the class.

20) Dozy

I sometimes felt a little high and other times even *dozy*.

The big Thanksgiving dinner left us all feeling satisfied and *dozy*.

After I ate a big dinner, I felt *dozy*.

I hardly slept last night. When I attended the lecture, I dozed a lot, *nodding off* during the lecture.

21) Dopey

Drugs make you feel very *dopey*.

Marijuana makes you feel *dopey/dopy*.

(cf. You are so *dopy*/stupid).

One of the Seven Dwarfs was called *dopey*, because he was a bit stupid not because he smoked *dope*.

Animals who feel secure and happy are *dopey* and relaxed.

The film is simply *dopey*, devoid of interest, and boring.

Obviously, making *dopey funny* films is his main source of cash.

Positive

22) Happy

I am not *happy* with your job.

If you are not *happy* with this work, then I will do it again.

Your performance so far is not satisfactory.

23)   Comfy

You need to wear *comfy* shoes to go on a bush walk.

(cf. Comfy is an abbreviation of comfortable).

Just be yourself, dress in what you feel *comfy* in.

Look at the *comfy* armchair.

They may look *comfy*, but surely he doesn't expect to knock in many goals wearing these

This area has been left deliberately blank for you to make notes or add other words.

Notes for Un/Satisfaction

3.1.3. In/security

Negative

24)   **Clingy**

Your baby is so *whingy* and ***clingy*** today. What's wrong with him?

My girlfriend is always ***clingy***. She does not allow me to <u>focus on</u> my work.

I need my own breathing space.

When a person becomes annoying by always wanting to be around you, s/he just basically suffocates you.

I see why Robert doesn't like Kelly. She won't leave his fuckin' ass alone. What a ***clingy*** bitch!

25)   **Fidgety**

The student looks very ***fidgety*** today, as he <u>looks bored</u> with his work and easily becomes nervous when I ask a question.

When your child is ***fidgety*** and <u>restless,</u> try to distract him with some form of creative dramatics.

With mobile phone abuse at a high, he can't help but get a little ***fidgety.***

Children can be very ***fidgety*** and not able to stay in one place or complete an activity.

Sit still and stop *fidgeting.*

- The baby starts to *fret/feel unhappy* as soon as her mother goes out of the room.
- The baby looks uneasy, restless and *fretful* when her mum is not around.

26)   **Edgy**

She has been very ***edgy*** and nervous lately.

She is always *on edge* before an interview.

When people receive criticism, they tend to become very ***edgy*** and defensive.

Too much coffee makes me ***edgy***.

Why are you so ***edgy?***

Their relationship has always been ***edgy*** and tense.

27) Nervy

Since the new professor was appointed, my director has become very anxious and *nervy* about any email I send.

To make a public speech is so *nerve wrecking*. It is very burdensome. I get very *nervy*.

The passengers were restless and *nervy* after the long flight.

Too much coffee makes me *nervy*.

28) Scary

The movie was so *scary**. You scare me.

For him, hurricanes aren't *scary*, they are simply frustrating.

Not sure that will happen, but it's a *scary* possibility.

It's got to be a *scary* time for them because the movie contains lots of violent scenes.

- You are a *scaredy-cat*.
- I almost never win, so I am too much of a *scaredy-cat* to enter the contest.
- You are not courageous. You are a chicken.
- I *feel scared of** the fire.
- I am afraid of you because you are a dangerous person.
- She is afraid of falling off the mountain.
- I am scared of jumping out of an airplane since I could die.
- I am scared to* speak German with your family because I might say something wrong and not know it.
- Have you ever been scared of the dark?

[Grammar 4: As you have noticed, when people express their emotions and feelings (AFFECT), then the Past Participle adjective form is used. However, when evaluating things (APPRECIATION), then 'ing forms of adjectives are used.

I am scared of	The movie is scary or scaring
I am tired of driving I am tired with him	Driving is tiring He makes me feel tired
I am excited about the trip	The trip is exciting
I am surprised at the story	The story is surprising
I am disappointed at your work	Your work is disappointing
I feel burdened and stressed when I have to do assignments	Doing assignments is stressful/ burdensome
I **am interested in** taking the course Students **take an interest in** engaging in the activity	Doing the course is interesting The course interests me
I **am concerned about** him I **am concerned with**	The situation is concerning The situation **concerns** me The task concerns me

29) Panicky

Whenever I hear an alarming sound, I become *panicky*.

When terrorists attack, the first thing you must do is *not panic*.

Stop being *panicky*.

Please calm down. Keep your composure in any *panicky* situations.

Go on the attack and she risks being labelled *panicky* and desperate.

That isn't being fearful or *panicky*; that is just good sense.

- *Panic attack* buttons are located on the top of the keypad.
- Sometimes moral panic can be created by certain individuals or groups.
- During Boxing Day, *panic buying* happened in David Jones.
- If you don't understand any of the terms above, *don't panic*.
- In *panic disorder*, the panic attacks may happen at any time.

30) Freaky

I was so scared of the dog. I hate dogs.

When I visited a friend of mine's house, the dog pounced on me. I was so *freaked out.* [cf. The terms 'scared of' and 'freak out' are almost the same but 'freak out' is an Americanism and is more associated with the drug culture of the 1970s].

I get so *freaked out* and *shaky*, when I see a car accident.

You *freak me out*. That is so *freaky*. The movie is so *freaky.*

The whole experience that I had in the country was really *freaky*.

[Cf. Freak has a different meaning. He is a movie *freak*.

My daughter is a *clean freak*. He is a computer game *freak*.

My ex-husband is a control *freak*, so I ended up getting divorced.

I think Nicole is a control *freak* - she asked Keith to stop singing country music].
Koreans are footy *freaks.* They have footy fever.

31) Guilty

I feel very *guilty* about what I did to her.

I don't feel any sense of guilt, because I am innocent. I have been falsely accused of this.

This area has been left deliberately blank for you to make notes or add other words.

Notes for In/Security

3.1.4. Dis/inclination

32)   Needy

When women start feeling ***needy***, the feeling inside makes them feel helpless and powerless. Then anything a woman does or says just radiates that ***needy***, desperate vibe. That vibe again just pushes men away even more. It's like we spiral downward, get caught in quicksand and find ourselves in an endless loop. Women <u>cannot figure out</u> how to pull themselves out of that situation.

She was so ***needy*** but she was also *greedy* that this tended to drive men away.

You have to help those who are ***needy.***

The Salvation Army helps <u>the ***needy*** or people who are in need</u>.

This area has been left deliberately blank for you to make notes or add other words.

Notes for Dis/Inclination

Unit 3.2. JUDGEMENT
3.2.1. Un/ethical (Propriety)

Negative

1)   **Bossy**

Nobody likes her, because she is very *bossy*.

Stop being *bossy*, otherwise you cannot <u>find favour in your teacher's eyes</u>.

She is getting *bossier* as she gets older.

That might seem just a little *bossy* to us.

She is a *bossy* older sister.

She has finally found her spot within the group and has even started to become a bit *bossy*.

The horse is quite *bossy* and likes to get his own way.

When I was little, my brother *bossed* me around.

- If I can <u>find favour in your eyes</u>, I will do everything for you.
- The little brat is the teacher's pet.
- This is my favourite child.

2)   **Bully**

The *bully* <u>bosses you around</u> at school.

School bullying is a serious concern for all educators.

The guy is a terrible *bully*. He is quarrelsome and <u>overbearing</u> all the time.

I quit my job because I was being constantly *bullied* by my boss.

I recently have lodged *a bullying complaint* form against my supervisor.

When you are *bullied*, you need to <u>stick up for yourself</u> by saying firmly and confidently "Stop it".

When the hooligans *mugged* him, he fended them off by doing Taekwondo. He is so brave.

If you are raped, don't hide it. You need to <u>pluck up the courage</u> to tell the police what happened to you. You need to <u>stand up for</u> yourself.

- He is so mean and cruel. [cf. 'Mean' has other meanings. Once I say it, I mean it. I don't say something for nothing. Mean also is a mathematical average).

  When you want to receive unemployment benefits from the government, you have to make an appointment with a person in social security. What they do is they check your income and do a means test to see if you are entitled to receive money].

3)   Bitchy

You are always so *bitchy* with me. I see how sweet and wonderful you are with friends, and with strangers, and yet you seem to save all *the bitchiness* for me. Why don't you just treat me the way you treat your friends?

That's not fair. I am not always *bitchy* to you.

You are *such a bitch.*

My wife is *bitching* at me all the time.

She is *a bitch.*

4)   Nasty

My boss belittles me. He puts me down in front of people. He despises and belittles me. He is so *nasty*. Don't be offended by his remarks. Get over it. That is the way he talks regardless of who he is talking to.

Regardless of/irrespective of who they are, what they are doing, where they come from, you've got to accept the person as they are.

Irrespective of colour, you should treat people equally.

My neighbour has a *nasty* dog that keeps barking at me.

I hate this smell of rubbish. It is so *nasty.*

He is a *nasty* teacher.

She is downright *nasty* to those who disagree with her views.

Before we get a bit too *nasty* we should probably talk about what happened first.

A particularly *nasty* strain of the virus can make normally healthy people very ill.

All I needed was something to relieve the pain from some rather *nasty* mosquito bites which I acquired.

The child has *nasty* habits like biting his nails or picking his nose.

If you see the world as a *nasty* place with evil around every corner, guess what?

- She always <u>speaks ill of</u> others. She is always <u>backbiting</u> and gossiping.
- She has a big mouth. She is a <u>busy body</u>. She is an extremely *nasty* lady.
- My maths teacher is <u>picking on</u> me for some reason. He <u>keeps teasing me</u> in front of all my friends.
- I <u>get so annoyed</u> at his *nasty* attitude.
- He is a bit of <u>a teaser</u> today.
- <u>Stop teasing</u> me otherwise I am not going to <u>put up with</u> it anymore.
- I <u>cannot stand it</u> anymore.

5)   Snobby

In general, pommies are very *snobby/snobbish.*

Pommies refer to people from England. They are <u>so proud of</u> themselves.

No, I cannot agree with you there. <u>To some degree/extent</u>, everybody can be <u>arrogant</u> in different ways.

He tends to have a *snobbish* attitude. He is *snooty*. He <u>looks down on</u> people.

Snobby critics ironically make a very good living reviewing Hollywood movies!

Snobby people, they are so wrong!

The spinster is too *snobby and picky.* That is why she <u>has not been able</u>* to find <u>Mr Right</u> up to now.

[Grammar 5: Tense for double modals]

I can do this.

I was able to do this.

I have been able to do this.

I will be able to do this.

I must do this.

I had to do this.

I will have to do this.

Double modals:

I should be able to do this.

I might be able to do this.

I will be able to do this.

Modal in a passive form:

This can be done by me.

This must be done by me.

This should be done by me.

This **needs to be done** by me.

6)   Haughty

From what I have seen, they are so ***haughty and snooty.***

He is boasting all the time.

- He is <u>bragging about</u> nothing.
- I am not bragging, but I can be very resourceful.
- <u>Stop bragging.</u>

7)   Showy

Everybody stays away from him, because he is <u>showing off</u> all the time.

He is too smug and boasting.

He wears ***showy*** jewellery and clothes. He says like look at me, look at me!

He has a ***showy*** and expensive car.

8)   Cocky

I hit the target on my first three attempts. Then I got a bit ***cocky*** [cf. A cock is a male chicken. They walk around with great pride, as do people who are acting or feeling ***cocky***]

Americans look very *friendly/neighbourly* but in fact they are very *cocky.*

They are <u>arrogant</u> in fact.

My favorite comedian is Yu JaeSuk because he looks very *friendly and neighbourly.* I feel comfortable with him.

That bloke has become very ***cocky*** and <u>arrogant</u> after his promotion.

9)   Brassy

The criminal is very ***brash/brassy.***

He is <u>*brazen-faced and impudent*</u>.

Even though he <u>committed a serious crime</u>, he did not show any remorse to the victim. He acts as if he did not do that.

She is a bit <u>brash and audacious</u>.

It sounds <u>presumptuous/rude</u>, but can I <u>ask you a big favour?</u>

It might <u>be a big ask</u> but I would <u>appreciate it</u> if you could send it to me.

10) Naughty

You are *naughty* if you <u>muck around</u> in your class without studying.

Stop <u>mucking around</u> here.

Stop <u>mucking around</u>. <u>Get on with</u> your work.

[cf. You have <u>mucked up</u> my life. You have <u>screwed up</u> my life. My life is completely screwed up because of you. This photo is <u>mucked up</u>].

He is a *naughty* (a negative term) boy.

This is my present for you. It's small but it is from my heart.

You are a *naughty* (a positive term) girl, you shouldn't do that.

I <u>was told off</u> by my mother for my *naughty* behavior.

- I <u>was told off</u> by my teacher because I misbehaved during class. She scolded me harshly.
- I <u>was grounded</u> by my parents when I got home.
- I <u>will give you big trouble</u>/you will be in big trouble if you don't listen to me.
- You <u>will be grounded</u> if you do not behave yourself.
- I was scolded by my teacher because I <u>wagged</u> classes too often.
- He <u>was telling me off</u> in front of my classmates.
- I <u>play truant</u> these days because I hang out with bad friends.

11) Sleazy

She acts like a prostitute.

She could be hot and <u>sexy,</u> but she wears very *sleazy* clothes.

The man is <u>devious</u>.

He approaches you and tries to touch you. He is so *sleazy.*

He is <u>out to get you</u>. He is <u>hanging around</u> you all the time. Be careful.

12) Skanky

She is very hot but *skanky.*

She wears *skanky* clothes.

13) Flirty

She is a bit *flirty/flirtatious* whenever she sees men.

When women find sexually attractive men, they begin to flirt.

14) Seedy

A *seedy* pub is smelly and unattractive. You feel uncomfortable there.

We eventually found the place which turned out to be a rather *seedy* looking underground car park.

They blame a recent drop in theatre attendances on the impression that the West End has become *seedy* in recent years.

15) Kinky

He is a <u>pervert</u>. He must be *kinky*.

He is a *kinky* character.

He has a *kinky* taste in sex.

What *kinky* things have you done for your spouse/lover?

16) Horny

Teenagers get *horny* when they see porno movies.

17) Greedy

You ate the whole pizza. I don't believe it! You greedy pig! You are a *greedy* pig.

These are some real-world examples of *greedy* companies and individuals that put their own desire for wealth and possessions ahead of the needs of others.

These are all examples of *greedy* behavior. Any decision to take from others or to enrich yourself <u>at the expense of others</u> is an example of *greed* and is something that should be avoided at all costs.

18) Stingy

He is so *stingy* and he never spends any money on us. He is <u>a miser</u>.

The company was too *stingy* to raise salaries.

Until his redemption, Ebenezer Scrooge is the classical example of a very *stingy*, heartless miser.

19) Pushy

Don't be too ***pushy*** with your children <u>when it comes to</u> studying.

<u>It doesn't work.</u>

This washing machine does not seem to function properly. This computer is out of order. It does not work.

In general, Asian countries value education a great deal but sometimes parents are too ***pushy***. This <u>puts enormous stress on</u> children. That is no good. <u>What's the point of</u> pushing children like this?

You are too <u>harsh.</u>

Don't be too <u>hard on yourself</u>.

Don't be so ***pushy***. Leave me alone. It is hard for me to hear you say that I am ***pushy***. You are probably <u>feeling really pissed off at</u> me.

20) Nosey

Parents are too ***nosey*** as a result.

They <u>are too concerned with</u> *petty* matters.

- They <u>put/poke their noses into</u> all of their children's matters. They pry into their children's affairs and peep into their rooms.

- Children hate being told to do this and to do that by parents. This causes a reaction from children. Children often become rebellious.

- Keep your nose out of it.

- Don't <u>interfere with</u> them.

21) Granny

Mum, please don't be a ***granny***. I know what I am doing.

[cf. Granny is an abbreviation of grandmother. In contrast, <u>nanny</u> is a person who takes care of a baby. I have hired a <u>nanny</u> to nurse my baby].

- I am sick and tired of her *nagging like a granny*.

- She *keeps nagging* me for no reason.

- <u>Stop nagging</u> me.

- I *feel disgruntled* when my boss asks me to do administrative work.

- I *get really annoyed* by my mother-in-law's nagging.
- She *is really a pain in the neck*.
- She is such a pest. My child *keeps pestering* me to buy the clothes.
- <u>Sorry for pestering</u> you but may I ask you a favour?
- Sorry for <u>bothering</u> you, but can you spare me a minute.
- <u>What bugs/bothers me is that</u> he did not reply to my messages.
- I <u>don't bother much</u> about that.
- Flies really annoy us when we have a Barbie[#] in the park in Australia. [cf.'Barbie' is an abbreviation of 'Barbecue' (BBQ). Let's have a barbie on the weekend].
- It *really irks* us and we feel irritable.
- They are *disgusting*. Snakes are really *disgusting*.

22)   Snappy
Stop being **snappy**. That's good for nothing.

Positive

23)   Thrifty
He is **thrifty** and *frugal*.

My mum never wastes leftover food. She thinks that <u>chucking</u> food <u>away</u> is so wasteful.

<u>What a waste</u> if you <u>chuck</u> food <u>away</u>!. <u>Chuck away</u> this rubbish.

She is economical. She has to *scrimp on* toilet paper and shampoo to save money.

We *scrimped* and saved to buy our first home.

24)   Worthy
I don't feel **worthy** enough to receive this award.

I am not **worthy** enough to pray to God.

It is not *worth investing* money in this. It is *not worthwhile to* invest money in this.

It is <u>no use doing</u> this. What's <u>the point of</u> doing this? I cannot see <u>any point in</u> studying hard.

25) Friendly

He is so *friendly*. He is warm-hearted, affectionate, and compassionate.

He has a big heart so you can lean on his big shoulders. He takes in everything I say. He is a very affectionate person.

The child is very *smiley*. Whenever I see him, he always smiles and gives me a big hug.

We received a *hearty*/big welcome from him when we visited his house.

He is so generous and hospitable. Thank you for your hospitality.

I feel like having a *hearty* meal at this time.

26) Lovely

My daughter is so *lovely*.

What *lovely* weather! It is *sunny* today. Beautiful.

This story is so touching and I was touched so much by his *lovely* present.

The couple are *lovey-dovey*.

- Some couples get along very well like a house on fire.
- But other couples fight like cats and dogs.

27) Homely

My daddy is very much a home body. He always comes home after work.

His landlady is a kind and *homely* woman.

The restaurant has a *homely* atmosphere. So I feel at home whenever I go to the restaurant.

28) Motherly

She is so *motherly*. Whenever I want to eat food, she serves me all the time.

The Asian lady in the restaurant is a kind and *motherly* woman, because she helps me to eat fish that has lots of bones.

This area has been left deliberately blank for you to make notes or add other words.

Notes for In/propriety

3.2.2. Un/truthful (Veracity)

29) Dodgy

The car mechanic is very *dodgy*.

He <u>ripped me off</u>. He overcharged me for repairing my car.

He is <u>untrustworthy</u>. He is <u>unreliable and unscrupulous</u>.

He is a bit of a *dodgy* doctor. He is <u>a quack doctor.</u>

The chair is a bit *dodgy*. Don't sit there.

30) Shoddy

He is a *shoddy* tradesman. He did a *shoddy* job. He cheats people because he charges money that he does not deserve.

- People are always <u>ripped off</u> by him.
- I realized that I <u>got ripped off</u> when I compared the money I paid for the bag with the money my friend paid.
- He is a <u>crook. He is dishonest</u> [cf. This knife is crooked /bent].
- The police chase crooks.
- I feel <u>crook</u> today, can I <u>have an *early* mark</u> today.
- All right I will give you a break. You can <u>have an *early* mark</u> today. But <u>one string/condition is attached</u>; you must do your homework. That's <u>fair enough</u>.
- He is <u>so crook</u> and he has to spend the night in hospital.

31) Tricky

He is a <u>conman,</u> but you would not know it. He is so deceptive.

He is very *tricky* and he looks like <u>a conman</u>.

I am going to use *a trick* to catch a thief.

He <u>conned</u> you by using *a trick*.

You <u>got conned</u> by the mechanic, because you were overcharged.

The essay questions can be very **tricky**. I do not know how to answer the questions.

I am in a <u>catch twenty two situation</u> at the moment, because I have no idea what to do.

When are you going to marry?

That's a very *tricky* question.

That is the <u>64 thousand dollar</u> question at the moment.

32) Flimsy

He is telling a lie. He is so transparent. He always makes a *flimsy* excuse when he is <u>in trouble.</u> That's a very bad attitude. He needs to <u>fix it up</u>.

Could you <u>fix up</u> this tap, it has been leaking since last week.

You cannot build a boat only from tree bark. It would be too *flimsy*.

33) Iffy

The meat smells a bit *iffy* to me. It must have gone off.

The student cannot attend the class, because his mother was sick.

It sounds a bit *iffy* to me. It is suspicious. He must be telling a lie.

I am doubtful/skeptical about his excuse.

Your man stops being *iffy* with you and tells you he loves you; then he does things that show otherwise.

34) Fishy

He is a questionable character. He is so suspicious. Something *fishy* is happening with him.

 He must be a spy.

There must be something *fishy* going on/around here

<u>Own up</u>/confess.

Who did a fart/did someone pass wind? <u>Own up</u>.

35) Quirky

He has some unusual quirks in his personality. He is a bit *quirky.*

He has a *quirky* sense of humour.

Did you see the program? It was a *quirky* TV show.

36) Grubby

Go and wash your *grubby* hands.

Some floor cushions look a bit *grubby* because children sit on them.

I went back to sleep, feeling slightly *grubby.*

We'll look very *grubby* indeed, won't we, <u>*in comparison to*</u> him?

37) Scabby

He is always begging for food here and there at lunchtime. He is ***such a scab***.

In these days, many men <u>sponge off</u> women like parasites. They are ***scabs/scabby***.

38) Sneaky

The tradesman deceives us secretly.

He is so *sneaky*. You can **sneakily** get out of here.

High school students *sneakily* watch m/X-rated videos.

The *sneaky* boy slipped outside to have a smoke without getting caught by his parents.

Once you get <u>caught red-handed</u> you will be in big trouble.

City people tend to be *sneaky.*

They are <u>city slickers</u>, while we are <u>country bumpkins</u>.

39) Speedy

Rats are so *speedy* and *sneaky* you <u>can hardly</u> catch them.

Don't *speed!* Don't drive over the speed limit, you can <u>get fined.</u> When I stopped in a non-stopping area, police approached me and <u>booked</u> me. I <u>got fined</u> $100. [cf. the weather is perfectly fine].

I was booked by the police. (cf. Can I <u>book</u> a room in your hotel?)

40) Crafty

He is very *crafty* and cunning/deceitful. He is so calculating.

I love doing *crafts*. He is a *crafty* man.

I hate my ex-wife so much because she was <u>sly</u> like a fox. Ex-husband, Ex-boyfriend, Ex-member. In Aesop's fables, 'the fox' is *crafty*.

This area has been left deliberately blank for you to make notes or add other words.

Notes for Veracity

3.2.3. In/capable (Capacity)

Negative

41) Geeky

School friends are <u>making fun of</u> you by saying you are **geeky.**

S/he is a <u>square </u>so s/he looks **geeky.**

Most scholars tend to be <u>pedantic</u>. They tend to <u>knit-pick about tiny details</u>.

Most of them are **geeky** .They do not have <u>well-rounded personalities</u>.

They have <u>their heads in the air</u>. They are not <u>down to earth.</u>

He is <u>a down to earth kind</u> of person.

I am still <u>up in the air.</u> I am still confused.

42) Nerdy

He only focuses on his study. He is *a nerd.*

My husband is *a kind of nerd*. He is a boring person. He is only interested in computers.

He also wears **nerdy** clothes that do not look fashionable.

If you are too serious about your study in Australia, you *get teased* by your classmates <u>rather than</u> get praised. S/he is a <u>machine</u>.

It sounds <u>odd/weird/strange,</u> but it is a fact of life.

It is so <u>weird</u>. It is really <u>warped</u>.

43) Airy-fairy

The politicians give **airy-fairy** descriptions in their political promises.

Blonde girls tend to have **airy-fairy** ideas.

They are <u>superficial, light and flippant</u>.

44) Wishy-washy

Most students have **wishy-washy** thinking that they will pass their subjects without putting in due efforts. These students <u>are likely to</u> fail in their studies.

Did he agree or not? It is hard to say. He gave a very **wish-washy** answer.

I loved this series but can't help thinking that this **wishy-washy** final episode lets the side down a bit.

The date techniques will help women handle their **wishy-washy** noncommittal man.

I recently realised that I like black music, but up until then I'd been a bit **wishy-washy.**

Knowing what you want is hot; if you're not **wishy-washy** a woman knows she's desired.

He *is inclined to* do the work. He has an inclination to_____

He *intends to* *study overseas. He *has the intention to* study overseas.

He *tends to* come late. He *has a tendency to* come late.

He *is likely to* come late.

Japan is likely to have an earthquake.

[Grammar 6: To infinitive or 'ing form]

Verbs that express desire or inclination only require the use of the 'to infinitive' and not an 'ing form. Examples are, 'tend to', 'is willing to', 'intend to' 'wish to', 'want to', 'hope to'. Other verbs of probability such as 'is likely to', 'appear to', 'pretend to', 'seem to' also require the use of the 'to infinitive' only.

The following examples of 'capacity' also are followed by the 'to infinitive' only.

I **manage to** complete my assignment.

I **attempt to** go overseas by myself.

I **cannot afford to** buy the house now.

I **decide to** attend the workshops.

He **offers to** give money to me but I **refuse to** accept it because it is considered to be bribery in my country.

I **neglect to** do the work, so I **deserve to** receive only a small salary.

However, the following inclination expressions require using 'ing forms or nouns rather than the 'to infinitive': be subject to/be prone to:

The area is subject to flooding.

The timetable is subject to change.

The country is prone to having earthquakes.

Japan is an earthquake prone country.

ESL learners are prone to making these grammatical errors.

I am a very *wishy-washy* type of person.

Don't be *wishy-washy* and make a careful plan <u>in advance</u>. You need <u>to preplan</u> it.

Don't make <u>an ad hoc</u> decision. You will face the consequences. You will <u>face the music</u>.

Think ahead/hard before you make any serious decisions.

45) Willy-nilly

Do not put the books *willy-nilly* on the bookshelf. Put them in alphabetical order. (cf. originally willy-nilly meant hesitantly, but now it means in a disorganized manner without direction or planning).

When the student went to his first week in university, he started joining clubs *willy-nilly*.

I can't find my keys or my wallet because I just leave things scattered about *willy-nilly*.

Politicians need to restrain themselves. They keep spending money on projects *willy-nilly*.

46) Clumsy

Most students are *clumsy* in using references when they first start their studies at university.

The job was done *clumsily* by you. I am very bad at doing this job.

My husband is very *clumsy* when <u>doing the dishes</u>.

A *clumsy* person always drops and spills things.

47) Hasty

You tend to always be *hasty*.

Don't <u>make haste.</u> Don't rush. Don't *hurry*.

He is always *in a hurry*. He is never relaxed. He needs to <u>take a rest</u>. I am *in a hurry*. I've got to go. I have to <u>hit the road</u>. Please take your time. Slow down.

I <u>used to</u>* work really hard, but now I have had to <u>slow down due to problems with my health.</u>

Do not make a *hasty* decision.

[Grammar 7: Use, used to (To infinitive), get use to ('ing form)]

I **used to live** in Seoul. Seoul is <u>one of the biggest cities</u> in the world. The <u>hustle and bustle</u> of the city is quite <u>overwhelming</u> at first. However, once you <u>get used to it, you will love it</u>. When I first visited a big market in Korea, I was so impressed. I love the <u>hustle and bustle</u> of the market.
But I did not like Korean food at first because too much hot chilly **is used** in the food, but once I **got used to** <u>eating</u> it, I loved it.

In the following examples**, to** is a preposition, so it is followed by the **-ing** form. Therefore, don't use a verb in the infinitive after the following expressions:

I **look forward to** <u>seeing</u> you soon.

I **devote myself to** <u>doing</u> this.

I **make strong commitments to** <u>attending</u> the workshops.

I have many **objections to** <u>transferring</u> his course at the moment.

Technology has **contributed to** <u>improving</u> our lives.

A positive aspect of education is that it **contributes to** <u>confirming</u> one's identity.

Positive

48)   Brainy

He is very smart and *brainy.*

He is <u>dumb and thick</u>.

I like *scholarly* people.

49)   Savvy

Generation Y has been characterised as media and internet **savvy,** as they have practical knowledge of how to handle computers very well.

He is a computer **savvy.**

50)   Handy

He is a *handyman*. He can fix everything. He is useful as he is a <u>go-getter.</u>

One thing that I like about Korea is that everything is so *handy.*

Shops are open late at night so you can get access to shops conveniently.

In Australia, shops close early. Sometimes, it is <u>a real hassle</u> to drive to buy food.

- <u>What a hassle!</u> It is a real <u>nuisance!</u>
- What a <u>nuisance!</u>

  I always carry a pen in my handbag. It often comes in *handy.*

  I received a bath towel as a present. That will be *handy.*

51)   Sassy

She is so **sassy.** She looks slightly sexual.

New Yorkers are **sassy** and confident**.**

52)   Witty

He is very **witty** and humorous. He loves to joke.

You are joking/kidding.

Witty is *funny* in a clever way.

This area has been left deliberately blank for you to make notes or add other words.

Notes for In/Capacity

3.2.4. Ab/normal (Normality)

Negative

53)   Fussy

My mother-in-law is very *fussy*.

The school excursion is still three weeks away but my son has already been *making a big fuss* about it.

My husband also *makes a big fuss* about small things.

They always <u>make a big deal out of nothing.</u>

Don't *make a big fuss* out of nothing. Why are you <u>making a big deal</u> about it? That's no big deal. He is making <u>a storm in a teacup.</u>

My arm hurts. It got bruised. Please put cream on my arm.

Ouch. Don't be *fussy*/don't overreact.

I am not *very fussy* about correcting your grammar <u>at this stage.</u>

54)   Finicky

My girlfriend is so *fussy and finicky* all the time so we broke up.

I <u>was dumped</u> by my boyfriend.

We <u>broke up</u> a couple of weeks ago but we <u>made up</u> soon after.

It is very *finicky* to fix up this resume.

-   If you want to get a good job, the first thing you need to do is to polish your CV (Curriculum Vitae).

55)   Picky

My son is too *picky/choosy* with his food.

My *hubby* is so <u>fastidious.</u> [cf. hubby is an abbreviation of husband].

<u>When it comes down to</u> buying clothes, I am very *choosy*/**picky.**

He is usually <u>laidback</u> but <u>when it comes down to</u> money, he is very *picky* and critical.

Australians are usually <u>laidback.</u>

<u>When it comes down to</u>*learning English,</u> there are no short cuts.

[Grammar 8: Focusing on items or things (GRADUATION: FOCUS)]

Moneywise, he is so critical.

As far as money **is concerned**, he is so critical.

With regard to money,

With respect to money,

With reference to money,

Regarding money,

Concerning money,

In relation to money,

Relating to money,

Focusing on money,

In terms of money,

When it comes to money,

56)   Choosy/Choosey

How is your <u>job hunting</u> going? You cannot be too *choosey*.

I have to be very *choosy* at this time when I am job <u>hunting/trying to find a</u> job.

57)   Loopy

He will *go loopy* when he hears the news.

My boss will be *loopy* and <u>furious</u> when I refuse to do the work he has asked me to do.

I tried to reassure him that I'd be okay, but I was already acting *loopy* from the poison.

I use the term '*loopy*' to mean strange, not acting normally, *crazy*, as 'in the guy was a bit *loopy*'.

Let's examine how *loopy* logic leads to *loopy* behavior when we allow our primitive and emotional brain to deal with worry without the help of our rational brain.

58)   Loony/Looney

They are *loony/crazy* as their behaviour is strange.

In the movie Hulk, the man *goes loony* when the moon changes.

He must be *a loony* because he grins at everyone.

Somehow, people who fight for rights and justice always get labelled with silly names such as '*loony*' and `eccentric'.

Every family includes someone who's a little *loony.*

The bull *went loony* when he saw the red flag.

- I just hit the roof because I was so upset about what he said.

59)   Crazy

I *go crazy* when my wife <u>keeps demanding this and that</u>.

- She is very demanding. Doing assignments in Australian universities is very demanding and challenging.
- The crowd went *crazy* when the Beatles stepped out on stage.
- She is *crazy* for him.
- He drives me nuts.
- I am just <u>out of my mind</u>.

- I am <u>beside myself</u> with anger.
- I <u>go mad/nuts/bananas</u>.

60)   Wacky

Wacky means *funny* or amusing in a slightly *crazy* way.

Some of his friends are pretty wild and *wacky* characters.

That motive was really *wacky* and strange.

The question is, <u>*why on earth*</u> would rational, sane and sensible people be so influenced by weird and *wacky* stories?

If you think this sounds a bit *wacky*, I'd have to agree.

He has *gorgeous* hands, with some really *wacky* silver rings.

I searched the web in an attempt to choose a school that didn't seem too *wacky*.

61)   Touchy

I can understand your feelings but you are so ***touchy/sensitive*** and you are the type of person who <u>gets easily offended/hurt</u> by little things.

<u>The way he talks</u> is very <u>provocative</u>.

I don't like <u>the way he thinks.</u>

He <u>stirs me up</u> and I get <u>so upset</u>.

When I feel like <u>enough is enough</u>, I <u>hit the roof</u>. I <u>lose my temper.</u>

I <u>am about to</u> hit the roof/I am <u>about to</u> explode.

He <u>is about to</u> go. He is <u>on his way</u>. He has just gone.

I was <u>almost about to smack/</u> hit her but I stopped.

62)   Shy/coy

The Greek couple are very <u>outgoing, sociable and gregarious</u> (get along well) but the daughter is unusually ***shy*** and **coy.**

Don't be ***shy***.

Don't b<u>e ashamed of</u> yourself when you make a mistake speaking English.

What a shame! It was a terribly shameful/disgraceful experience.

63) Dreamy

The girl is such a *dreamer*. She is obsessed with a Hollywood actor.

He is so **dreamy**, she says about him**.**

Teenage girls have lots of pipedreams. They tend to imagine that they will be swept away by a knight in shining armour. 'Be realistic'. 'Come on, get real'. 'Wake up to yourself'. These days, contrary to our expectations, girls are the ones who pick up the boys. [cf. Pick up has several meanings. I need to pick up my English. The economy is picking up. I will pick you up. Please pick me up at seven].

64) Sissy

The boy is a **sissy.** He cries like a girl.

The other kids laughed at him and called him a **sissy** because he didn't like sports.

The candidate touts his wartime service as evidence that he is not a **sissy.**

65) Cheeky

The baby is getting **cheeky**.

You are a **cheeky** boy. Look at that **cheeky** face. Are you playing a game with me? Such a **cheeky** boy!

66) Rowdy

I have **rowdy** neighbours. They are very *noisy*.

In Australia, you can usually make a big noise when you have a party at the weekend. Other than the weekend, you've got to be careful, you need to have a chat with your neighbours beforehand. Otherwise, they will report you to the police.

- If you come across North Korean spies, please tip off the police. Please report this to the police.

- Other than that/apart from that, everything is ok for me.

Positive

67) Chatty

My wife is quite *chatty* and talkative.

She is a very *chatty* person.

Can I *have a chat* with you? Can I have a word with you?

Let's have *a chit chat* at the weekend.

He is usually quiet but when it comes down to *footy* games, he becomes very *chatty*.

68) Bubbly

We were greeted by two very *bubbly* members of check-in staff working on the counter.

The people we see are nearly always *bubbly*, and *giggly*.

My husband is usually very quiet but *when it comes to* political issues he becomes very *bubbly*.

69) Tidy

My husband's personality is totally the opposite of mine. He is a *tidy and orderly* type of person but I am very laidback and *untidy*.

The wheelie bins look quite *tidy* along the lanes.

He has **a** *tidy* appearance because he refrains from drinking alcohol.

The house is in *a tidy* condition for the next occupant.

70) Funny

The American is so *funky*. The clothes he wears, the way he acts and speaks is so *funny*.

I watched a comedy yesterday. It was so *funny*.

It was a *funny* story.

Believe me. After you graduate there will be so many girls for dating. It is not *funny*.

Funnily enough, he denies his mistakes.

It is so *funny* and I was cracking up so much It felt like my *tummy* was about to burst.

- You crack me up. I have a *tummy* ache. My *tummy* is aching.

71) Customary

It is very *ordinary/normal* that children bow to their parents during New Year's holiday or Thanksgiving Day.

That's the *usual* condition.

It is **customary** that he acts like that. It is customary behavior.

This area has been left deliberately blank for you to make notes or add other words.

Notes for Ab/normality

3.2.5. Un/determined (Tenacity)

Positive

72) **Steady**

He studies very *steadily*. He is so <u>serious and studious</u>.

He is *steady* and stable.

- This will serve him in good stead in the long run.

- Learning to use a computer will serve you in good stead.

- Boys tend to be less tenacious than girls. They cannot keep their bums on their seats. They are easily distracted.

  The couple has a *steady* relationship.

  Now I have a *steady* job.

  There is a *steady* table in the house.

Negative

73) **Scatty**

<u>Pay attention to</u> the ball when you play tennis.

You <u>make the same mistakes</u>.

You are so *scatty*. You are thoughtless.

In general, girls are more <u>tenacious</u> than boys. That is why girls usually excel over boys.

Boys tend to be *scatty*. They don't care much. They don't <u>concentrate on</u> their work much.

74) **Silly**

That's *bloody* (extremely) stupid and *silly*.

Your behaviour is *silly*. Don't be a *silly billy*. He is a *silly* boy.

You are behaving in a slightly *silly* way today.

75)   Lazy

He is so *lazy*. He watches videos to <u>kill time</u> instead of studying.

He is **a *lazy*** bum**.** He is so <u>slack</u> these days. Your work is so <u>slack.</u>

- You have arrived so early. You are *an early bird*.

- There is an old proverb that says an *early bird* catches the worm.

- *Early bird* registrations for the conference can get discounts.

- The *earlier* the better.

- First come first served. I have been <u>slack</u> lately.

- It is <u>such a fluke</u> that he won the lotto.

- He passed the most competitive exam. <u>What a fluke!</u>

- It was <u>just a fluke </u>to have received such a highly contested scholarship.

- It is an unexpected windfall. It is such a <u>fluke</u>.

- They are determined to show that their last win was <u>no fluke</u>.

76)   Tardy

You will be courteous if you leave room for someone who might be just a bit ***tardy*** because of traffic.

Generally speaking, people are ***tardy***/slow to act in paying their bills.

77)   Lousy

You are so *lousy* and **sloppy.** You need to <u>pull your weight</u> more.

He is a *lousy* player.

He is a *lousy* manager, because he did not reply to my emails.

This is a *lousy* piece of work.

This is *lousy* weather.

Even if the proposal contains *lousy* strategies, I am going to read it.

78)   Sloppy

My daughter is so *lazy* and ***sloppy***. However, my son is a <u>hard worker.</u>

Young people's English is a bit ***sloppy***. He did a ***sloppy*** job.He said: "the players have to know that I will not stand for things being too ***sloppy*** for too long.

This area has been left deliberately blank for you to make notes or add other words.

Notes for Tenacity

Unit 3.3. APPRECIATION

3.3.1. Un/appealing (Reaction)

It is concerned with whether people **like or dislike something** and whether **things grab people's attention or not.** Reaction can refer to **people and things or facts.**

To describe people's appearance

1)   Shabby

She wears *shabby* old jeans. She is poorly dressed.

The old man looks *shabby* and s*cruffy.*

You look very *shabby* today.

2)   Bushy

I had my hair cut today, because my hair was so *bushy*.

I have become *bushy* of eyebrow, grey of hair, dry of skin, plump of middle.

You have a *bushy* beard.

3)   Spiky

After I got my hair cut, I realised that my hair style was too *spiky.*

I don't feel comfortable with that.

He was quite tall and buff and had *spiky* brown hair.

The thorn trees look suitably *spiky* and you certainly know not to land on them if you can help it.

4)   Cutey

The baby looks so *cute.* You are such a *cutey*. He is gorgeous. He is a good looking guy. Look at the little girl. She looks like a doll.

She is very nice, but she's not afraid to *get cute* when there's something that she wants.

An example of a *cutey* is a charming little girl in pigtails with whom everyone is delighted.

5)   Chubby

I feed him very well. His face looks so *chubby*. The baby is <u>plump</u>.

Move your ass, *fatty*.

Don't eat too much *fatty* food.

Look at the fat lady! Her arms are so *flabby*.

6)   Skinny

You have become so *skinny*. You are so <u>slim</u>. Look at your *boney* arms!

I enrolled at a gym/fitness club/sports centre last year.

Since then, I have been exercising very hard to make myself fit and *healthy*.

Don't do too much exercise. Like taking drugs, exercising is also addictive. You have

become a <u>gym junkie</u>.

7)   Muscley

My favourite movie star is Song Il-Guk. He looks so cool, and so handsome. He is also so

muscley/muscular.

8)   Manly

He can look so *manly* when he lifts heavy stuff. I have never been drawn to a movie star

like him.

The female singer has a *manly* voice.

The male singer sang a *girly* song.

9)   Sporty

He is *sporty*. He likes all types of sports.

He is so big and *mighty*. He has a big build.

10)   Perky

Look at the model. She is so hot and *steamy*. She is so vigorous and *perky*. Her nipples are

perky.

My husband is already out of steam.

He used to be full of steam. He is not strong any more. He is over the hill.

Reaction is also used for **assessing things, processes and entities.**

This can be divided into several subcomponents.

Describing food

11)   Greasy

Chinese food is usually very *oily* and **greasy**, whereas Japanese food is simple, mild, bland and less *spicy*.

12)   Chilly

Korean food is usually very hot and *spicy*, because it has lots of chillies in it.

The food is too *salty*.

[cf. The weather gets crisp and **chilly** in autumn.]

In Autumn, when it gets cold, the weather feels **chilly** and crisp.

13)   Sugary

The food is too **sugary**/sweet.

Oils, crisps, sausages, pastries, fried foods (fatty foods), and sweets, cakes, chocolate and biscuits are all examples of *fatty* and **sugary** foods.

14)   Tangy

Mustard is **tangy**.

The Indian food has a **tangy** taste and flavour, a bit like rocket.

15)   Crunchy

I love potato chips because they are **crunchy** and *crispy*.

[cf. He is very lazy but when it comes to crunch time he performs very well].

The cabbage should be slightly *crunchy*, not soft.

Add the spring onions and remove the pan from the heat so that they remain *crunchy*.

16)   Junky/Junkie

Heroin *junkies* are wasting their lives.

That's all <u>junk</u> food and rubbish.

17)   Chewy

The meat is not tender/soft and it is very *chewy*.

The Chinese cabbage is very *watery* because it is out of season. Korean people like *watery* soup.

The cooled caramels will be soft and *chewy* at this temperature.

When mixed with eggs, they create a soft custard base with *chewy* lemon pieces and a pleasantly bitter edge.

18)   Yummy

My wife is a good cook. Look at the food she cooked.

Yum, beautiful. It is so *yummy*. I am already <u>drooling</u>. <u>Stop drooling</u>.

Serve over *fluffy* rice to soak up every last drop of the *yummy* sauce.

Almonds and cinnamon make this chocolaty beverage *yummy*.

Unsweetened coconut and *yummy* spices make this curry truly fulfilling.

I love Korean barbecue. It is really *tasty*.

- Can you give me some tips on how to cook?
- The secret is that you need to marinate with the right seasoning.
- Your seasoning is just right. I am good at seasoning.
- While I am good at cooking, I am poor at hiking.

19)   Yucky

Korean food is very *yummy* but that soya bean paste is still too *smelly* and *yucky* for me.

While the food is delicious to you, it is <u>tasteless </u>to me*.The water was *dirty* and smelled *yucky.* I felt *yucky* after eating all that cake.

[Grammar 9: Concession (While, although, even if, even though, despite, in spite of, nevertheless, albeit) (ENGAGEMENT: Countering)]

- <u>While</u> I am willing to help (Positive +), I do not have much time available (Negative -).
- <u>Although/even though/even if</u> he worked hard (+), he failed in the exam (-).
- <u>Albeit</u> he worked hard, he failed in the exam.
- **Despite** his working hard, he failed in the exam.
- **In spite of** his working hard, he failed in the exam.
- **Despite the fact that** he worked hard, he failed in the exam.
- He worked hard, <u>but</u> he failed in the exam.
- He worked hard. <u>However</u>, he failed in the exam.
- He worked hard. <u>Nevertheless</u>, he failed in the exam.

Albeit is often used to introduce an adjectival or adverbial <u>phrase</u> that makes a concession about the preceding <u>noun</u> or <u>verb</u>. For example:

- His speech was impressive, <u>albeit</u> rather short.
- She appeared on the show, <u>albeit</u> briefly.
- It was an amazing computer, <u>albeit</u> expensive.
- The lesson was interesting, <u>albeit</u> difficult.

20) Tasty

The food you cook is really *tasty.*

Tundra cabbage is surprisingly *tasty* and tender for an over-wintered cabbage.

I don't *have access to* *my server as I use shared hosting, but robot cop sounds very *tasty*.

[Grammar 10: Transitive verbs]

Access (verb/noun), get access to.

- If you **have access to** the internet, you can gain useful information from it.
- Drag the icon to the desktop for easy access (noun).
- This is partly due to the lack of direct access (noun) from ward pcs to the hospital pharmacy.
- However I have been unable to access (verb) the basic setup screen to configure the gateway to access (verb) the internet.

21) Sticky

Australians don't seem to like *sticky* rice cake.

This is a *sticky* situation means that this is a difficult or unpleasant situation.

I have *sticky* fingers.

The room has *sticky* surfaces.

22) Savoury/Savory

The food is so *savoury.* I think the main distinction is just between sweet and *savory,* and sometimes people use the terms loosely.

A *savory* food can also be *salty* or *spicy*, but generally a sweet food isn't and just leans toward the *sugary* side. I think a *savory* food usually has some "flavour" though, *as opposed to* simply leaving the sugar out of something.

Compared with *Korean food, Australian food is less *salty*.

89

[Grammar 11: Comparison (ATTITUDE: APPRECIATION)]
'Compared to' and 'Compared with'

Both prepositions, **to** and **with**, can be used following **compare**. Neither is more correct than the other, but a slight distinction can be made in meaning. Firstly, **Compared To** has traditionally been preferred when the similarity between two things is the point of the comparison. On the other hand, **With** suggests that the differences between two things are as important as, if not more important than, the similarities.

- Life has been **compared to** a pilgrimage, **to** a drama, **to** a battle.

- Paris has been **compared to** ancient Athens.

- Congress may be **compared with** the British Parliament.

- Paris may be **compared with** modern London.

- I hesitate to compare my own works **to** those of someone like Dickens.

- We compared the facilities available **to** most city-dwellers with those available to people living in the country.

Secondly, while '**with**' is used for generalisations, '**to**' is used to compare statistical facts:

- A four-by-four uses more fuel **compared to** a mini.

- Compared *with* the Victorians, we are a much healthier society.

- **Compared with** Australia, China is much cheaper when it comes to commodity prices.

- **Compared to** South Korea, Australia is 50 times larger in terms of its size.

- For example, if you're graduating from high school you can go straight to college, **as opposed to** taking a year out of school and working.

23) Juicy

The fruit is so *juicy*. It is <u>succulent.</u>

We had *juicy*, delicate king fish with a good coating of subtle native spices.

The only rule is not to add wet ingredients, such as tomatoes, which are too *juicy*, otherwise the pizza becomes *soggy*.

We had *juicy* gossip about one of the contestants, Michelle.

24) Slimy/Slimey

The eels are very *slimy*.

I hate eating raw octopus. It is too *slimy*.

If you pick some of it out of the water, you will notice that it has a slightly **slimy** feel.

Toads are not *slimy* or *warty* and do not jump like frogs.

The sea creature was huge, *hairy*, and very *slimy*.

25) Soggy

If you put tomatoes in a sandwich, it gets *soggy* and *sloppy*. I don't like it.

Take care to clear up all the shattered pieces – they become very *soggy* on melting.

Soggy soil is a clever ecological solution for shade lovers.

In the living room the curtains smell like birds' poo and are all *soggy* and wet.

Describing places such as rooms & houses

26) Dusty

Your room is so *dirty*. The windows are so *dusty*. Look at the dust on the furniture.

27) Messy

Your room is so *messy*. It <u>stinks</u>. It is *stinky*.

It is <u>gross</u> and repulsive. Please *tidy up* your room.

Does the presence of customers make the shop look *messy*?

She has *messy* handwriting.

They have been through a *messy* divorce.

28) Filthy

The shanty towns are very *filthy* and *dirty*.

When you travel by train, you can see that stacks of rubbish are littered around the railway.

It is an eyesore. Your room is so *dirty* and *untidy*.

Every time I see your room, I frown.

Your hands are *filthy*. Go and wash them immediately!

29) Grotty

The rubbish bin is *grotty* and *smelly*.

Redfern is a *grotty* part of Sydney.

Lack of sleep not only makes you feel *grotty*, it leads to a suppression of the immune system.

From the outside, the upper floors looked fairly *grotty* but the ground floor was quite grand.

It is a standard hospital, quality-cheap and basic according to some, pretty *grotty* according to others.

30) Smelly

Your room is *smelly* because your carpet is so old. It is so *musty*.

That is gross and disgusting.

Yuck. Your feet are *smelly* and gross.

Get the job done very quickly and the tray doesn't get **smelly**.

31) Musty

Houses in Australia are very dark. They are *musty* and damp.

It is very damp and humid especially during the *rainy* season. Many houses get moldy because of the humidity.

Inside we found a slightly *musty* pub with walls covered with beer mats.

Don't feed hay which is *dusty*, or smells ***musty***.

The straw should smell sweet, not ***musty*** or stale.

32) Murky

The water in the swimming pool will get ***murky*** if you do not put chemicals in during the summer.

The afternoon was *cloudy* with a slight shower later and became ***murky*** toward evening.

With all these hidden cards, things can get pretty ***murky.***

Today was very ***murky***. I was surprised the picture came out at all.

33) Muggy

What is the weather like in Korea? Korea has four distinct seasons. The summer is very hot, humid and *sticky*. The summer is *rainy* when we have the rainy season. In summer, the weather is so <u>damp</u>.

It is a bit ***muggy*** outside.

Describing places and movies

34) Creepy

The movie is a bit ***creepy.***

The big doll looks ***creepy***.

I heard some strange noises. It was pretty ***creepy.***

Despite the weak ending, there are some genuinely ***creepy*** moments in the film.

This would be enough to make anyone feel ***creepy***.

35) Seedy

The street is <u>eerie</u> because it has many ***seedy*** bars.

Most people on the ***seedy*** street look under the influence of drugs.

Either way, it's a very ***seedy*** way of marketing.

We eventually found the place which turned out to be a rather ***seedy*** looking underground car park.

36) Spooky

The movie is *spooky.*

The strange man lives in a *spooky* and *eerie* old house.

My mum used to tell me *spooky* stories at bedtime.

While the sound is fuller, the effect is to make the lyrics even more *spooky*.

37) Gory

Spartacus is a *gory* movie. It involves* a lot of blood and violence.

I do not like these types of movies.

It's brutal in places, *gory* in places, and supernaturally *creepy* in places.

Perhaps a little too *gory* was the inclusion of a bowl of human ashes in the exhibits.

The movie contains lots of violence and *gory* scenes.

[Grammar 12: Transitive verbs: involve]

- I **was involved in** the court case.

- Change management **involves** planning, implementing and evaluating changes in an organization.

- Many people **are involved in** the incident.

- The scope of this position may **involve** some evening and weekend hours.

- I did not want to **involve** him in what we were talking about.

- Many university students **are engaged in** part-time work.

Describing weather

38) Foggy

On our way to the mountains, it was freezing cold. It was so *foggy* and *misty*, we could not drive.

My memory is a bit *foggy*.

In the morning, it gets *frosty*.

It is likely to be *stormy*. We had a *stormy* discussion.

It is too *foggy* in front of me, I cannot drive.

When a bushfire occurs, all the cities become *smoggy*.

The sky in Hong Kong is always *hazy*.

The room is very *smoky* because many people smoke cigarettes inside.

39) Nippy

It is a bit *nippy* today, because of the strong wind.

[cf. look at the *nippy* little sports car. The car moves very quickly and easily.]

40) Windy

Today is very *windy*. It is very *windy* today (cf. The street is windy, not straight).

41) Snowy

I love to go to a *snowy* mountain.

The winter here is not as *snowy* and *icy* as South Korea. However, you feel <u>much colder</u> than in South Korea.

42) Sunny

When it is **sunny**, it gets warm.

When it is *cloudy*, it gets cold. The sky is overcast today so it feels much colder.

Describing colour

43)   Greeny/greenish

Bluey/pinky/yellowy colour.

Describing landscape

44)   Slippery

The road is also **slippery** too.

When the floor gets wet, it becomes so **slippery**.

When you walk into a swamp, it is so _muddy_.

45)   Hilly

This street is very **hilly**.

He lives in a **hilly** suburb.

46)   Stony

This mountain is very **stony**. It has **a stony** hill.

Describing other things/clothes/furniture

Positive

47)   Cuddly

The teddy bear doll is so _snuggly_ and **cuddly**.

This blanket makes me feel _snuggly_.

Give me a **cuddle**/hug.

Give me a big hug.

48) Cosy

Your house is so *cosy,* like the house in the story of Snow White and the 7 dwarfs.

I like a *cosy* room.

49) Fancy

Your car looks so nice. It looks so *fancy.*

North Sydney is a <u>posh</u> area.

People living in that area are so *classy* and <u>posh</u>. They buy *fancy* furniture.

- You are too extravagant given your income.

- Your home is too luxurious considering* your income.

- Provided* that you have enough income, you can buy a house now.

- When you buy a house, you need to make allowance for/take into account/take into consideration your ability to repay.

[Grammar 13: Allowance (ENGAGEMENT) - Considering, make allowance, given that, etc.]

'Given the fact' implies it is proven, it is verifiable.

'Given that' means when you consider the following...

- I gave her a promotion **given the fact** that she is a good employee.

- It was surprising the government was re-elected, **given that** they had raised taxes so much.

- **Given/considering** his age, he is remarkably active.

[Grammar 14: Condition) - provided and providing: ENGAGEMENT]

The words provided and providing are interchangeable when used to mean 'on condition that'.

Examples:

- **Provided that** the weather is fine, we'll have a picnic on Saturday.

- **Providing that** the weather is fine, we'll have a picnic on Saturday.

- Tony will attend **provided that** Sarah is not chairing the meeting.

- The newspaper did not publish the photographs because they were given by a confidential source who gave them **provided that** we did not release them before the elections.

No Need for 'That': The word 'that' can be omitted.

Examples:

- **Provided** the weather is fine, we'll have a picnic on Saturday.

- **Providing** the weather is fine, we'll have a picnic on Saturday.

- You will be awarded a prize **on the condition** you complete the course.

- His reasoning is **based on the premise** that all people are equally capable of good and evil.

50) Lively

I love this city because the atmosphere is *lively*.

I enjoyed the *lively* rock concert.

The football match was *lively*.

51) Trendy

Designer brand bags are very *trendy*. They are <u>stylish and fashionable</u>.

They are currently very popular among young ladies. But I reckon it is just a <u>*passing fad*</u>.

Having a tattoo is <u>*just a passing fad*</u>.

He is a very <u>refined and cultured</u> person.

52) Fluffy

The cushion that I bought the other day is very *fluffy*.

I am an eight year old lady with a very *fluffy* tail!

I love rabbits too. They are so *fluffy* and loveable.

Negative

53) Flashy

In Thailand, every souvenir looks *flashy*.

I just want a good reliable car, nothing *flashy*.

He specializes in *flashy* technique, without much depth.

The actress was *flashily* dressed in the movie.

Evaluating people's appearance

54) Tacky

You look very *tacky* when you wear these jeans.

They are <u>out of fashion</u> now.

When you buy *tacky* souvenirs, you will be bored with them within the week.

For me, Indian movies are a little loud and garish; quite *tacky*.

Some look great dressed up, others just look *tacky*.

55) Crappy

What a bunch of *crap.*

This work is completely *crap.*

It is a *crappy* novel. It is full of rubbish.

Her jewellery looks very *crappy.*

56) Saggy

After women undergo breast feeding, there is tendency for their breasts to become *saggy.*

Being exposed to the sun can make you old before your time – making your skin look *saggy*, *wrinkly* and *leathery*.

He is however a little *saggy* in this picture *due to*[*] *it being* a hot day.

[Grammar 15: Causes and effects - Causative verbs (ENGAGEMENT)]. This is a very important grammar, particularly in writing.

- **Due to/because of** the rapid development of the internet, users can gain new knowledge conveniently.

- **Due to/because of the fact that** the internet has been developed rapidly, users can gain new knowledge conveniently.

- **Since/As/Now that** the internet has become prevalent, users can obtain updated information easily.

- The internet **enables** users **to** <u>access</u> new information easily.

- The internet **allows** users **to** <u>get access to</u> new information efficiently.

- The internet **helps** users **(to)** retrieve new information conveniently.

- This will **help (to) achieve** your goals.

- The internet **assists** students <u>in doing/to do</u> their assignments conveniently.

101

57) Baggy

Your jeans are too *baggy*.

If *Baggy* packaging was not used on products then consumers would use little plastic baggies instead.

This fabric doesn't shrink, fade or go *baggy* even after frequent washing.

She always wears *baggy* clothes to hide her weight.

58) Daggy

They look so **daggy**. They need to be <u>hemmed.</u>

The lovely Kim Wilkins says this: "Everything that made me *daggy* and unpopular has turned out to be a blessing", and I couldn't agree more.

Yet it is clear that despite our internal self-perception that the Anglican brand is *daggy*, the average Sydneysider is actually very warm towards us.

The *daggy* clothes you are wearing look uncool, unfashionable, but comfortable.

The boring, *daggy* lesbian is the one associated with difficult, challenging politics.

This area has been left deliberately blank for you to make notes or add other words.

Notes for Reaction

3.3.2. Un/balancing (Composition)

It is concerned with **whether or not something hangs together, is balanced or complicated**.

1)   Cruisy

His life is so smooth and *cruisy*. He just *cruises* around.

He sat for the most difficult exam, but he breezed through it.

I have to *sit for* the college entrance exam.

He inherited lots of property/real estate from his parents.

His parents *handed him down* a means to a good income.

He is so *lucky*, because his life will already *be a cruise*.

He has a *cruisy* job.

2)   Fiddly

It is quite *fiddly* closing this necklace because the latch is so small.

Cooking Korean food is very *fiddly* and elaborate.

I hate sewing because it is one of the most *fiddly* jobs.

Making jewellery is very *fiddly*.

Please stop fiddling with the computer when I am talking to you, pay attention to me.

I have fiddled around to work on this paper.

3)   Wordy

You need to be working on your paper more. *Tidy* it up a little bit and hand it in next week.

When you write an essay, don't make sentences too *flowery* and don't speak in *flowery* language. It becomes too *wordy* and *lengthy*.

Lecturers hate Asian students' digressive and indirect ways of writing essays.

Stop rambling and wandering around. Get down to the point first.

4) Corny

Corny is often used to describe someone or something that wants to be cool, but isn't. It sounds childish/lighthearted/a joke/*silly* not *funny*. For example, if your friend got a tattoo on his arm and thought it looked really cool, but you thought it looked stupid, you could say that the tattoo looked *corny*.

I know it sounds *corny* but it really was love at first sight.

It is a *corny* movie.

He makes a *corny* joke.

It may sound a little *corny*, but I like to visit places where few can go.

It is so *corny*, but it's very hard not to shed a tear.

Adam Sandler's movies are really *corny*.

My brother tries to talk with a British accent, but he sounds *corny* because he's not very good at it.

I bought these *corny* shoes yesterday for Halloween.

5) Cheesy

Cheesy is a similar word to *corny*. The difference between the two is that something that is *cheesy* is trying very hard to be cool. A *cheesy* person is someone who thinks he is the coolest person in the world, when in truth he's a dork.

It sounds *cheesy* (superficial), but I try to express myself.

It is an incredibly *cheesy* love song (of low quality and without style).

The film is long and somewhat *cheesy*, but it is very informative.

6) Fuzzy

This is a *fuzzy* area. My eyesight is getting *fuzzy* as I get older.

You can see a couple of rather *fuzzy* photographs of them here.

I feel uncomfortable and my vision goes *fuzzy* fairly quickly.

7) Bulky

The parcel is so *heavy* and ***bulky*** that I cannot handle it by myself.

The bag is too ***bulky*** to carry with me at all times.

We have not had a chance to try one, but they do look a bit ***bulky*** and rugged.

It is difficult to flush away the ***bulky***, *greasy* stools.

8) Hefty

He needs to diet, as he is too *heavy*. Look at the Yudo player. He is so strong, *heavy*, and muscular. He is ***hefty.***

I have made a ***hefty*** decision today.

You are so big. How much do you weigh? I am very *heavy*.

I dropped four dress sizes from what was a pretty ***hefty*** 16 down to a 10.

I have to pay ***hefty*** fines because I parked my car without a ticket.

In 1995 mobile phones were largely a business tool and still too ***hefty*** for the average pocket.

9) Lofty

I will become a millionaire in two years' time. It sounds like a pretty ***lofty*** objective.

It is a ***lofty*** ambition. The house has ***lofty***/high ceilings.

It might be a tall order/demanding but could you finish the project by tomorrow?

10) Chunky

The pieces are ***chunky.***

Give me a ***chunk*** of the meat.

Porcupines are slow movers with their ***chunky*** round bodies.

It's still early days for e-readers, and consumers can only choose between a few ***chunky***-looking models.

If you do not like ***chunky*** tomato sauce, you'll appreciate the *finely* diced carrots in this one.

11)   Roomy

The kitchen is so *roomy*. It is so spacious.

The interior of the car is *roomy*.

The house has *roomy* drawers, shelf, towel rail and bottle storage bin.

The underwater passage is quite *roomy*, about 3ft square.

12)   Scanty

Your literature review is *scanty* and insufficient.

You need to do more literature reviews.

Her clothing is very *scanty*.

She is wearing *scanty* panties.

You have to drink plenty of water if you want to keep yourself healthy and fit.

Can I give you more? No that's *plenty*.

This water reservoir used to have *plenty of* water. Now it suffers from a lack of water because of the drought.

We should use water sparingly. I would really *appreciate it* if you could spare some time for me.

13)   Foamy

This soap is very *foamy*.

A foamy bath can help dissolve the natural body greases.

Foamy waves swelled and gave off vapour.

14)   Glossy

The wooden floor boards look so *shiny* and *glossy*.

Vogue is a *glossy* magazine. It has lots of ads for high-end products.

He brought a *glossy* brochure for his presentation.

15) Boggy

There are many reasons why a person may feel *boggy* (soft).

The house has *boggy* (soft and wet) ground.

The ground was *boggy* under foot.

16) Flaky

Fish have lots of *flaky* scales.

These biscuits are very *flaky.*

They would twist and crack, and their surfaces would become *flaky*.

I have a *flaky*, *itchy* scalp.

17) Prickly

This tree is very *prickly*.

When I tell a lie, it *pricks* my conscience.

When he *was falsely accused* because of my mistakes, my conscience *pricked*.

A cactus is very *prickly*.

I caught my foot on some rather *prickly* undergrowth which split the top of the boot.

She felt a *prick* as the thorn jabbed her foot.

He felt the *prick* of the needle.

18) Thorny

Thorny shrubs *deter** unwanted visitors *from* climbing over your fences.

The rose bush is very *thorny*.

It is a *thorny* issue, as it is a difficult topic for people to agree about.

This is proving to be a very *thorny* subject.

[Grammar 16: Negative causative verbs (ENGAGEMENT)]

- The goal is to **protect** healthy people **from** <u>developing</u> a disease or experiencing an injury in the first place.

- He should do more to **prevent** that **from** ever happening.

- They add that therapies designed to **prevent** this **from** happening during drug use could one day help to thwart chemical dependency.

- Procrastination severely **hinders** many people **from** putting their intentions into practice.

- Chewing gum may **stop** you **from** smoking heavily.

- Social Services and Health Commission services offer good support and help to **keep** people healthy and safe **from** abuse

19) Wobbly

The leg of the chair is *wobbly*. It moves and is unstable.

I have a *wobbly* tooth and hate the thought of it dropping out.

I feel quite *wobbly*, having heard first hand from him.

My car has *wobbly* wheels and I need to fix them.

20) Wonky

That painting hanging on the wall is *wonky*. You had better straighten it.

My face didn't go right back to normal, my smile is a little *wonky*, my eye seems a little smaller.

It is still important to get some good right angles or else the toy will still look *wonky*.

A *wonky* oak floor may lead to a furniture problem.

You have *wonky* teeth. They are crooked not straight. You have to get braces.

21) Wiggly

Worms are *wiggly*.

Little children get restless if they have to sit still for a long time and they get **wiggly**.

Her bottom *wiggled* as she walked past.

He removed his shoes and *wiggled* his toes.

22) Shaggy

My hair is too long and untidy. It is too *shaggy*. I need to have it cut.

The sheep dog has a *shaggy* coat of fur.

They had *shaggy*, thick wool and two horns.

My daughter has long untidy and *shaggy hair*.

23) Shady

We went to find somewhere cool and *shady* to have a drink.

We have a big tree in our garden. So the garden is *shady*.

He is a *shady* and *dodgy* character.

24) Shadowy

Someone was waiting in the *shadowy* doorway.

It was very difficult to see him because he was standing in a *shadowy* corridor.

He is a *shadowy* figure. He is a bit suspicious.

25) Leafy

Most streets in Sydney are very green and *leafy*.

North Sydney is a *leafy* area.

This area has been left deliberately blank for you to make notes or add other words.

Notes for Composition

3.3.3. In/significant (Valuation)

1) Pricey

This stuff is very *pricey*.

House prices have become very <u>dear</u> and expensive lately.

I saw a wedding on the London Eye and it looked fantastic, it wasn't too *pricey* either.

Unfortunately, live telephone support can get *pricey* in a hurry.

I can tell you, furniture is quite *pricey* over here!

2) Costly

It is so *costly* to raise a child these days.

I have made a *costly* mistake. It is a very serious mistake that causes long-term damage.

Climate change is therefore likely to have considerable and potentially *costly* implications for the UK.

It is so *costly* to maintain the house.

The policy is *costly* to implement at a national level.

However, getting an eco-scheme wrong can be extremely *costly*.

It will be very *costly* once the ecosystem is destroyed by the pollution.

3) Rosy

Life is not *rosy* all the time. It has its <u>ups and downs.</u> Don't think that the world always revolves around you.

Oh dear, things don't look too *rosy* for us, do they?

No one should have the illusion that everything will all of a sudden become **rosy**.

She has *rosy* lips and cheeks that every man loves.

You know things aren't all *rosy* for these kids.

4) Easy-peasy

It is child's play. That is **easy-peasy.** It is <u>a piece of cake.</u>

Can you play "Mary had a little lamb on the piano"? Of course, that's **easy-peasy**!

It is not easy* *to* live in foreign countries. You may face many difficulties. Life is not *easy*, and it becomes complicated.

[Grammar 17: ATTITUDE (APPRECIATION)]

When valuing things, it is common to use the dummy subject or object 'it'. For example:

- **It is** extremely/vitally/crucially **important** for me **to** speak English fluently in order to get a decent job in Australia.

- **It is essential/integral/indispensable** for international students to have a good command of English to complete their studies in Australian Universities.

- I **find it** very important to speak fluent English in order to get a decent job in Australia.

Others include such evaluations as easy/difficult, un/necessary, im/possible, un/natural, etc. For example:

- **It is very difficult** for first year students <u>to write</u> an essay.

- First year students **find it difficult** <u>to write</u> an essay.

- Unless your soil is very sandy, **it is not necessary to** add organic material**.**

- **It is apparent/clear/evident** that oil reserves will be exhausted by 2050.

Negative

5)   Rusty

Your car is old. It is *rusty* all over. You need to dump it. Get rid of it.

When it comes to playing the piano, if you don't <u>polish</u> your skills, they get *rusty.*

I need to <u>brush up</u> on my English.

6)   Rocky

The mountain is *rocky* with cliffs and the sandy bays are in coves rather than long stretches.

A **rocky** shore is an intertidal area of seacoasts where solid rock predominates.

Our relationship is getting *shaky* and *rocky*. We have a *rocky* relationship.

Our marriage is <u>on the rocks</u> means our marriage is not strong.

How is he doing since he joined your church?

Oh he is <u>rock solid</u>. His faith is very firm and strong, because he is a devout Christian.

- You shouldn't <u>rock the boat now</u>, you need to be patient.

7)   Risky

It is too *risky* to buy stocks now. You <u>run the risk of</u> losing all your money.

<u>Strangely enough</u>, this is true, although it's a somewhat *risky* practice.

In addition, they are right to do so, since relying solely on Russian gas and fair business conduct appears too *risky*.

- When it comes to buying stocks, you've got to be very prudent/careful/circumspect, otherwise you will end up losing all your money.
- They ended up divorcing.
- At the end of the day, you have to face the music/face the consequences.
- We gave you good service. But at the end of the day, you started to pass the blame onto us.

8)   Irony

It is such an **irony** that the ugly lady is married to a handsome man.

When she *married* him, he had no money. He is married with three children.

9)   Faulty

The electric device is ***faulty***.

Everybody has faults/foibles, weak points and strong points.

The problem is you might have a ***faulty*** perception of a situation.

10)   Leaky

Damage to blood vessels may cause inflammation, but may simply make blood vessels ***leaky***.

This tap is ***leaking***.

This gas pipe has rust everywhere. It can readily become ***leaky***.

The ***leaky*** roof is not being fixed by the council.

This area has been left deliberately blank for you to make notes or add other words.

Notes for Valuation

Section 4: Other expressions with Y

4.1. Common rhymes of abbreviations ending with Y

Y ending rhymes	Examples
Airy-fairy	He is an *airy-fairy* person. He is unrealistic. He has his head in the clouds. I've got my feet on the ground. While my husband has his head in the clouds, I am a down to earth person. '*Airy-fairy* bullshit' contrasts well with '*nitty–gritty*'
Argy-bargy	I am fed up with your *argy-bargy* way. It is too noisy and disruptive.
Hunky-dory	Everything will be *hunky-dory*. This means that everything will be fine.
Hurly-burly	The country is in a *hurly-burly* political situation
Hustle and bustle	City life has *hustle and bustle*.
Itsy bitsy or itty-bitty	I cannot explain the *itsy bitsy* details of the story now.
Lovey-dovey	I hate it when my mum and dad get all *lovey-dovey*. It is so embarrassing at their age.
Nitty-gritty	I have had enough of this superficial talk. Let's get down to the *nitty-gritty* of the issue. Let's get down to the *nitty-gritty* of the matter. The *nitty-gritty* of the problem is that he does not comply with the company rules.
Roly-poly	He is a really *roly-poly* guy, because he is very fat. The lollypop lady guides students to cross the road safely. Children like lollies.
Silly Billy	Don't be a *silly billy*.
Topsy-turvy	He went through *topsy-turvy* lifestyles.
Wishy-washy	Don't be so *wishy-washy*. Why can't you give me a definite answer?
Willy-nilly	Do not use your credit card *willy-nilly*. You should be careful. Hey! What are you doing with those seeds? You have to plant them in rows and evenly-spaced. Don't just toss them *willy-nilly!*

Other types of rhymes	Examples
Chit-chat	Let's have a **chit-chat** some other time. She is a very **chatty** person.
Claptrap	He talks a lot of claptrap and nonsense.
Chock- a-block	The bus was **chock-a-block**, I could not find a seat. The stadium was chock-a-block! It was a complete sell-out. You can imagine the atmosphere!
Knickknacks	The shop is decorated with many little **knickknacks**. I can't afford to buy anything but **knickknacks**.
Mishmash	Koreans like **mishmash** food. I like a **mishmash** of food. I have got a **mishmash** of an assignment.
Mumbo-jumbo	I think a lot of 'art talk' is **mumbo-jumbo**
Pitter-patter	The **pitter-patter** of little children running around a house. How long before I can hear the **pitter-patter** of little feet? Said by a pregnant woman to her obstetrician.
Riff- raff	They are **riff-raff** living in the slums.
Shipshape	Everything is **shipshape** in a Bristol fashion. My husband keeps things **shipshape**.
Tiptop	The house is in **tiptop** condition. You are now at the pinnacle of your life.
Tittle-tattle	I don't like office **tittle-tattle**. Women tend to engage in tittle-tattle gossip when they get together. **Chit-chat** relates to innocent gossip, while **tittle-tattle** relates to malicious gossip.
Tit-for-tat	The row was a **tit-for-tat** action.

4.2. Common abbreviations for nouns

Original words	Abbreviation (acronym)	Examples
Bad people	Baddies	
Barbeque	Barbie	
Bicycle	Bike	
Biscuit	Bikkie	
Breakfast	Brekky	
Bricklayer	Brickie	
Cat	Pussy	
Cigarette	Ciggies	
Dad	Daddy	
Dog	Doggy	
Electrician	Sparkie	
Football	Footy	
Good people and things	Goodies	
Grandmother	Granny	
Holiday	Hollies	
Hooligan	Hooly	
Husband	Hubby	
Mosquito	Mossie	
Mum	Mummy	
Nice person	Sweetie	
Old person	Oldie	
Politician	Pollie	
Sick leave	Sickie	
Soap operas	Soapies	
Surfboard rider	Surfie	
Television	Telly	
Umbrella	Brolly	
Underwear	Undies	
Vegetables	Veggies	
Woolworths	Woollies	

References

Burns, D. D. (2008). *Feeling good together*. New York: Broadwaybooks.

Butt, D., Fahey, R., Feez. S., Spinks, S. and Yallop, C. (2000). *Using Functional Grammar: An Explorer's Guide* (2nd ed.). Sydney: National Centre for English Language Teaching and Research.

Donaldson, R. M. (2011). Teaching foreign language conversation: A conversation norms approach. A Thesis California State University, Chico.

Eggins, S. (2000). *An introduction to systemic functional linguistics (2nd ed.)*. London: Continuum.

Halliday, M. A. K. (1994). *An introduction to functional grammar*. London: Edward Arnold.

Halliday, M. A. K. & Matthiessen, C. (2004). *An introduction to functional grammar*. (3rd ed.). London: Edward Arnold.

Hood, S. (2004). Appraising research: Taking a stance in academic writing. Unpublished PhD thesis, University of Technology, Sydney, Australia.

Hood, S. (2010). Appraising research: Evaluation in academic writing. London: Palgrave Macmillan.

Jones, G & Polly, P. (2013). Scafolding student learning by mastering the development of academic literacies through an oral assessment. In Coleman, k & Flood, a. (Eds). Marking time; Leading and managing the development of assessment in higher education, Champaign, Illinois: Common Grounds Publishing LLC.

Lee, S. H. (2006). The use of interpersonal resources in argumentative/ persuasive essay by tertiary students. Un published PhD thesis, University of Sydney, Australia.

Lee, S. H. (2007). An application of multiple coding for the analysis of ATTITUDE in an academic argument. *Journal of Linguistics and the Human Sciences*, 3(2), 165-190.

Lee, S. H. (2008a). The use of interpersonal resources in argumentative/ persuasive essays: Cross-cultural and grade-based differences between ESL and Australian tertiary students. VDM Verlag Dr Müller, Saarbrücken, Germany.

Lee, S. H. (2008b). An integrative framework for the analyses of argumentative/persuasive essays from an interpersonal perspective. *Journal of Text and Talk*, 28(2), pp. 239-270. DOI 10.1515/TEXT.2008.011

Lee, S. H. (2008c). Attitude in undergraduate persuasive essays. *Journal of Prospect*, 23(3), 43-58.

Lee, S. H. (2010a). Command strategy by balancing authority and respect by undergraduate students. *Journal of English for Academic Purposes.* 9(1), 61-75. doi:10.1016/j.jeap.2009.11.001

Lee, S. H. (2010b). Attribution in high-and low-graded persuasive essays by tertiary students. *Journal of Functions of Language.* 17(2), 181-206. DOI 1a 1075/fol.17.2.02lee.

Lee, S. H. (2010c). Differences in the use of Appraisal resources between L1 and L2 writers: Focusing on GRADUATION system. *Journal of Issues in Intercultural Communication ,*3 (1).21-47.

Lee, S. H. (2013). An evaluation on a team teaching by university students and lecturers in Australia. *Journal of Language Teaching and Research*, 4(5), 914-923. Doi: 10.4304/jltr.4.5.914-923.

Lee, S. H. (2014). Argumenta structure as an interactive resource by undergraduate students. *Journal of Linguistics and the Human Sciences,* 9(2), 273-299, doi: 10.1558/lhs.v9i2.273.

Martin, J. R. (2000). Beyond exchange: Appraisal systems in English, In S. Hunston and G. Thompson (eds.), *Evaluation in Text.* London: Oxford University Press, 142–175.

Martin, J. R., & Rose, D. (2003/2007). *Working with discourse. Meaning beyond the clause* (1st/2nd ed.). London and New York: Continuum.

Martin, J. R., & White, P. R. R. (2005/2007). *The Language of evaluation: Appraisal in English.* (1st/2nd ed.). London and New York: Palgrave/Macmillan.

Thompson, G. (2013). *Introducing functional grammar*. (3rd ed.). London & New York: Routledge.

Further Help & Purchasing the Book

1) Author website: Help and advice can be found here:

- http://susanshin.wordpress.com

2) Publisher: You can find out where to get further copies of this book here:

- http://www.cranmorepublications.co.uk/student

3) Book stores in Australia:

- http://www.thenile.com.au/books

- http://www.coop.com.au

- http://www.booktopia.com.au

- http://www.fishpond.co.uk

- http://www.inbooks.com.au

- http://www.newsouthbooks.com.au

- http://www.palgravemacmillan.com.au

4) Espresso Book Machine:

- The Co-op Bookshop Custom Book Centre, Melbourne

5) US, UK, France, Germany, Italy, Spain, Canada:

- http://www.amazon.com

- http://www.amazon.co.uk

- http://www.amazon.fr

- http://www.amazon.de

- http://www.amazon.it

- http://www.amazon.es

- http://www.amazon.ca

6) Free worldwide delivery (including South Korea):

- http://www.bookdepository.com

7) Bulk Orders:

Discounts are available for orders over 20 copies. Please email cranmorepublications@gmail.com for details.

8) There is a companion book which is aimed at teachers rather than students. It contains more theories about communication from a linguistic perspective:

Principles and Practices of Oral Communication: Appraisal Theory and its Application to Casual Conversation

http://www.cranmorepublications.co.uk/student

9) Contact the author:

susanshin713@yahoo.com.au   or   sook09@hotmail.com

If you know of any other 'Y' expressions which could be included in the book, or if you have any comments or feedback, then it would be great to hear from you.

Thank You

✎ Test yourself!

Commonly used words that end in 'Y'

Please read through the following expressions containing commonly used words that end in 'Y' to see how many you know and use in everyday conversation. Simply tick the relevant column. If you tick less than 10 boxes in Column 1 then you need to consider buying this book.

	Column 1	Column 2	Column 3
	I know and use it in everyday conversation	I understand but I never use it	I don't know the expression
She is a very **bossy** woman.			
My neighbour tends to be **snobby.** They do not like to mix with people from other backgrounds.			
My 5-year-old boy is very **fussy.** He does not eat any vegetables.			
My husband is a very **finicky** person, while I am quite **laidback.**			
He's got a **quirky** sense of humour. Not everyone finds his jokes funny.			
Children usually get very **cranky** when they are not fed.			
He is very **grumpy** today for some reason.			
She is very **stingy.** She only gave me a card for my birthday.			
He is such a **jolly** guy.			
That mechanic is pretty **dodgy.**			
She is very **nasty.** So everyone hates her.			
He looks so **geeky** with those thick glasses he wears.			
There are all these **brainy** people at university.			
She usually wears **tacky** clothes.			
When the alarm bell rings, don't get all **panicky**.			
There are some pretty **freaky** people on Oxford Street on a Saturday night.			
It is very **fiddly** to make this kind of jewellery. You need very steady hands.			
Total			

How many boxes did you tick in Column 1?

1-5 (   )   6-10 (   )   11-15 (   )   More than 15 (   )